Dust and Dragons

Rob Jacques

Fernwood
PRESS

Dust and Dragons

©2023 by Rob Jacques

Fernwood Press
Newberg, Oregon
www.fernwoodpress.com

All rights reserved. No part may be reproduced
for any commercial purpose by any method without
permission in writing from the copyright holder.

Printed in the United States of America

Cover image: "Nine Dragons" by Chen Rong, 1244 CE

ISBN 978-1-59498-099-2

Rivers and mountains all empty clarity: there's a road in,
but caught in the dust of this world, I'll never find it again.

— Su Tung-p'o

This book is dedicated to

Delia J. LaPointe
&
Emily D. LaPointe

who raised me from the dust and taught me
how to behave when I encounter a dragon.

Table of Contents

Preface 11
Dust and Dragons 15
Once Upon a Time 17
Dust Versus Dragons 19
Rubáiyát 20
Our Role 22
Thacher Island, Rockport, Massachusetts 23
Voices 25
A Good Day 27
World Inside 29
Great Misery Island, Salem Harbor, Massachusetts .. 30
Love in Time 32
Koan 33
My Boyfriend is an Asian Dragon 35
Stardust 36
Coronavirus 37
Ambient Air 39
May You Live in Interesting Times 41
Dust Mites 42

... They Moved Together
  Through Dust and Dragons 43
Beatitude 1 45
Beatitude 2 47
Beatitude 3 48
Beatitude 4 49
Beatitude 5 50
Beatitude 6 52
Beatitude 7 54
Beatitude 8 55
I, Dragon 56
Disbelief 58
COVID-19 60
Consciousness on the Way 61
My Grandmother Busies Herself in My Kitchen 62
There Be Dragons 64
Simplification 65
I Am Who I Am 66
Why the Night Sky Is Dark 67
Milky Way 69
Orbis Non Sufficit 70
A Dragon Speaks 72
Adagio for Alpenhorns 74
Centripetal Versus Centrifugal 78
Idleness 80
I'm Tidying Up Things
  With My Grandmother Again 81
Angst Astride a Dragon 83
Adagio for Timpani 85
Before Dust Settled 87
Memory of a Shadow of a Fog 88
What Will He Get? 90
Gold Dust 91

Hey, Billy	92
Adagio for a Young Cousin	93
Old in a Dust Storm	95
Sequel	96
Spring Dreams in Autumn	97
Dragonfly	99
Ars Moriendi	101
Adagio for the Oort Cloud	102
Dusting	104
Incarnations	106
Youth's Departure	108
Congenital Myopia	109
Those Who Knew Me	
When My World Was Young	111
Winter Dragon	113
Immortality	115
Being in a Garden	116
Purgatory	121
Intellect as Companion	122
Last Illusions	124
Hymn to Yesterday's Gods	125
It's Not Dementia	128
Auld Lang Syne	130
What If It Comes as a Sleeping?	132
. . . And They Lived Happily Ever After	133
On Your Finding I'm Gone	134
Heroic Crown of Sonnets:	
Ancient Chinese Poets	135
1	135
2	136
3	137
4	138
5	139

6.	140
7.	141
8.	142
9.	143
10.	144
11.	145
12.	146
13.	147
14.	148
15.	149
Acknowledgment	150
Title Index	151
First Line Index	155

Preface

Ancient Chinese poets saw each person as a consciousness moving through space and time, and they surmised the Cosmos to be an infinite and eternal flux of the physical and the metaphysical—a mixing, stirring, churning river of immortal, eternal, infinite flow. They realized the five senses were poor tools indeed to use in comprehending reality and all its roiling phenomena, but they also felt each human was an integral part of existence and was subject to nature, an observer of nature, and a part of nature.

These poets, whose experiences and art span centuries, grasped that the ultimate understanding of all things comes from within oneself and that clarity could be found in this world through meditation, observation, humility, simplicity, friendship, and love. Wine, conviviality, and laughter now and then also go a long way toward lubricating the process.

We wake to reality, gain insight to our place in the Cosmos, and become aware of our own abilities when we stand apart from the flow of daily life and embrace the natural world in rural and undisturbed settings. This is why ancient Chinese poets often applied rivers and mountains as metaphors for clarity of vision, along with clouds and mist for intellectual and creative mobility and fluidity in this world. Awake and aware, we really see. The Cosmos comes clean; we realize absence, emptiness, and hollowness are not instances where something is missing but are instances pregnant with possibilities, with becoming, with promise waiting to be fulfilled.

Enter human frailty. Unawake and unaware, humans produce dust. Their meaningless hurry, accumulation of useless wealth, development of spurious beliefs, waste of space and time, pursuit of fame and reputation, and chasing after pointless goals are all dust that prevents them from clearly seeing reality all around them, enfolding them, and controlling the flow of all things. Usually we do not see this dust constantly falling throughout our daily activities and settling over everything of value to the point where we cannot recognize even the surfaces of existence or the truth of the Cosmos.

What's to be done? Well, the ancient Chinese poets found an answer in stepping aside from the human fray and intellectually dusting off their lives through self-reflection, active participation in the flow of nature, and meditation on the origins and destinies of all things. The profound and artistic results of their efforts rest in their poems.

And then there are those dragons for which we must account: powerful, protective, snake-like, lion-fierce, lightning-clawed, chaos-causing, storm-rousting, reality-arousing Chinese dragons that both appear and disappear with equal suddenness and violence. These are not your evil, stereotypical dragons of the West breathing fire and imprisoning damsels in distress. They are not like Fáfnir slain by the Norse hero Sigurd, nor are they so easily treated as those encountered by Great Britain's St. George, nor are they like the 50 that cowardly and callow Gawaine dispatches in Heywood Broun's marvelous tale, *The Fifty-First Dragon*.

No, these are metaphysical— not fairytale— Chinese dragons, and they demand attention, fear, and respect. Intricately woven throughout five millennia of Chinese culture, they cannot be ignored, cannot be outmaneuvered, and cannot be slain. They are intimately associated with water, and they lurk in China's ponds, lakes, rivers, and oceans, and sometimes even evolve out of and devolve into mountain clouds and valley mists leaving behind destruction, creation, desolation, division, unification, insurrection, revelation, and apocalyptic experiences, as well as enormous opportunities . . . for those who are worthy.

The ancient Taoist philosophers and poets were familiar with these dragons, paying them homage in their meditative musings and poems and explaining to people wise enough to understand the flow of space and time that dragons are indifferent to the fate and interests of humans, their actions being inscrutable and random manifestations of their creative, destructive, and protective urges. Earthquakes, floods, typhoons, conquests, landslides, civil unrest, and fortune both good and bad are indications dragons are on the move, bursting forth from their watery lairs into space/time and the affairs of human beings. They shake up landscapes and dynasties. Their actions are not destructions or desecrations, but merely waves and cataracts in the flow of the material universe, and although unpredictable, they are almost always opportunities for the enhancement of human enterprise if seen in the right light and used by skillful minds to advance their interests. The Chinese dragons are frightening, dangerous, and beautiful, but they mean people no harm. The swift-thinking person can see in their thrashings and churnings the creation of possibilities of use to those who follow the Way and respect the power of change.

And so the following poems present both the human passions and predicaments of involvement with dust and dragons, passions and predicaments that cannot be avoided, only observed and endured. Or grasped and turned to advantage. Dust and dragons: ambiences of the human condition. Dust and dragons: metaphysical realities along the Way, first out of and then back into Oblivion.

Rob Jacques
Winter 2023

Dust and Dragons

*Life is made of limits,
but understanding is limitless.*
— Lao Tzu

Throughout space/time it falls, coming down
softly, relentlessly, simultaneously everywhere
humans do their dirt: business, government,
school, church, or town, everywhere, everywhere
falling, coating, covering human help or hurt,
falling invisibly through the air, through the mind,
falling, hovering, gliding, coming to rest inert
on surfaces of reality where humans labor blind.

See it resting on passion. See it lying about
on love. On hope. On promises and prospects
formed in the heyday of youth before doubt
became the norm for all tomorrows— dust
in its infinite, immemorial numbers a silent rout
of the five ineffectual senses, intellectual rust.

But there be dragons. Throughout space/time
they rise, writhing up out of all the world's waters
into atmospheric, geographic, apocalyptic change
where abiding dust flashes off splashed surfaces,
dust previously hiding all things pure and strange,
dust grievously smashed and cleansed away by
dragons, dragons making us awake and aware
painfully, frighteningly, of our being only clay.

See a dragon scale shimmer wet, sparkle bright,
the thrash of a tail sweeping away complacency,
the slack of a lower jaw drooling opportunity
for those alert to how igniting chaos gives light
by which to climb above desolation, desecration,
to find other famished flesh to know and love.

Once Upon a Time...

The Big Bang of my birth exploded a universe,
put me in it, eyes opening for a first time on love,
five senses, one by one by one by one by one
brightening, heightening, enlightening consciousness
and acclimatizing me to space/time's danger and fun.

I saw a smile for the first time and I lay awhile
in the arms of innocence, in the hands of simplicity,
imagining in my early moments mile-on-mile
of the flow and fluctuations of life's river ahead,
the experience, the sharing, the finding, the felicity.

There was crawling, toddling, walking, and running
ahead of me, and once control of my body was mine,
there would be creation. Accretion. Adhesion.
And then there would be accomplishment, stunning
discoveries of myself, finding myself pliable, benign.

On those first lush days flushed with sun and sheen
dust was nowhere on my horizon, nor it did cloak
the fine ways I threaded between seen and unseen,
known and unknown, heard and not heard, dust being
an adult thing like my having to submit to the absurd.

I understood birds and their necessities were mine:
food, sunlight, safe nests, company, warmth, and song.
All my waking was spent enjoying my five senses
and playing beyond the clutches of right and wrong,
winging myself toward where entropy commences.

All day I rode in the pleasuring sky of friendly clouds
that whitened or darkened and I, wind-tossed with them,
sailed my magic existence forward toward crowds of
promises and praise I knew would be mine by evening,
everything hot with temptation that never, ever strays.

And in imaginative night, soon to be lascivious night,
delicious night, inconspicuous night, night which lovers trust,
I found sleep came too late to stop my body's learning,
to kill my slowly corrupted mind's callow yearning.
In bed I found bare beginnings of what would end in dust.

Dust Versus Dragons

If heaven and earth can't make things last,
why should we humans try?
   — Lao Tzu

The dust we kick up in our blitherings and ditherings
settles for eternity on all we would do and be,
all things transitory hidden under its constant descent.
It clings to us and we cannot shake ourselves free.
It obscures the fair, the honest, the true. It won't relent,
won't depart, won't spare a surface from its debris
covering, coating, smothering, leaving us content
to while away a lifetime never really awake or aware.

Enter the dragon. Unexpectedly, it rises from its lair
slithering amok and awry up and out of the status quo,
and it will soar and it will roar, scattering addling dust,
shattering ego and pride and other fallible human rust,
bringing chaos, slinging change in each startled face,
all that dust, dust, dust whisked away without a trace.

Rubáiyát

The Moving Finger writes; and, having writ,
Moves on: nor all your Piety nor Wit
Shall lure it back to cancel half a Line,
Nor all your Tears wash out a Word of it.
   — Edward FitzGerald

The river of space/time flows on and away,
its cataracts and eddies mixing night and day,
consciousnesses becoming and coming undone,
appearing, disappearing in arcs of work and play.

Mortals find its waters as shallow as morning dew
though they splish and splash about in petty stew,
not comprehending their passage down a stream
that only shortens, darkens, and does not renew.

Mortals focus on fear, anger, greed, and lust,
not on being kind, giving, introspective, and just,
and they float unaware of the river's destination,
unawake to their world inevitably becoming dust.

Mortals buy glittery baubles at life's brief bazaar
to deceive themselves as to what they really are,
playing with time, playing for time, playing games
to avoid knowing their lives are circling a dying star.

The child who comes into space/time pure and clean
soon forgets, regrets, and upsets the golden mean
on the river's lifetime ride back to original oblivion
where what five senses detect is no more to be seen.

Only the elderly freighted with experience understand:
gargantuan wrenchings of birth and death command
all that flows in between on the river of space/time
and that everything humans build is built on sand.

Let your narrative turn to sensual poetry, line by line,
and may you pause where love was, drink some wine,
and laugh at the swiftness of the present becoming past,
the sweet brevity of consciousness, humanity's and thine.

Our Role

> *We have not arrived to explain, but to sing.*
> — Kim Stafford

We have arrived at planet Earth, our destination,
without explanation, minus instruction, lacking a guide.
We disembark the dark womb without trepidation,
minus wisdom's solace, lacking a course in the tide
that carries us onward, awkward, forward toward
a return to wherever exists outside of space/time
whence we came, bringing nothing, taking nothing,
learning in the interval— we hope— something sublime.

Sing we will of the joys of mortality, its youth, its age,
its running commentary by five senses that tells truth
if we but learn how to read its languages in life's rage,
and sing we will as we go down, sing of space/time
as we flow in its epiphanic river, aware, awake, children
of oblivion, for oblivion, looking back with a lover's ache.

Thacher Island, Rockport, Massachusetts

Granite shelves rising to just below
murky surfaces lie slyly just offshore
of an Atlantic surf, lie in the tidal flow
in apocalyptic wait with nary a warning
for unwary souls to come near and founder.

Oh, sure. Look now from a calm shore,
from the safety of a Rockport harbor jetty,
from the sanity of summer's still waters
before fall storms, the profanity of winter's
blizzards hazarding civilization's norms.

The low island lies menacingly athwart
the harbor's mouth as if a thing alive,
a dragon guarding a New England port,
and Samuel de Champlain saw in 1605
how it beckons sailors as if in sport.

Captain John Smith saw in 1614 how
the island reckons with vessels too close
to its submerged shelves to allow safe
passage, an island replete with ruin
for those who can't see hell's deceit.

But Anthony Thacher and his wife saw it
as the only people to survive a wrecking,
haunted ever after by what they endured
one gale-driven night on island rocks:
cold, wet, frightened, and death-taunted.

For centuries, stone-towered twin lights
marked this island's danger, only a fool
approaching from seaward on low tides
when a ghost of granite hides just below
a gray surface lying silent, calm, cruel.

Today we row through danger to picnic,
laugh and dance, play at hiding, unaware
of the panicked, the drowned, the dead
whose bones rot at our feet, the remains
of sailors' forgotten stories abiding there.

Voices

And have you heard voices?
I've heard them calling my name.
Is this the sweet sound that calls the young sailors?
The voice might be one and the same.
  — Paul Williams & Kenneth Ascher

In my bedroom's midnight quiet, I hear them.
In the pause of my held breath before shouting
for love, for mercy, for merciful understanding,
I hear them. I hear them in my disturbed sleep
and when there's a pause in my day's demanding.

Rivers and mountains are the company I keep,
and their voices are those of eagles and breezes
that course through valleys and sky— voices
interminably mingling with a murmur, a heartbeat,
a cry, voices singling me out from humanity awry.

They speak to me of long-ago centuries at rest,
once buoyant and floating, but now somnolent,
stilled on the bed of the river that is space/time,
once filled with pulses, breathing, love-making,
and love lost, but now ethereal if once sublime.

They speak and reality glistens with their sound
that can only be heard with imagination, belief,
awareness of eternal passages through infinity,
consciousnesses speaking to a consciousness
now moving beyond the five senses in its seeking.

The dust of this world does not make one deaf.
The dark of this world does not make one blind.
The world's song is carried by voices in my mind
speaking to me in seasons, over decades, on call
whenever I slow and step aside my ego's treasons.

"Eternity is in this moment," the voices say, and
"You are always. What has been will be again.
You are us; we are you; we and you will love again
in oblivion. It's true: the river of space/time eddies
into oceans to renew its rise to the skies with you."

A Good Day

May this day come ad nauseam,
again and again repeating incessantly,
seconds redone hour on hour, mornings
recurring, afternoons so similar they pall,
evenings repetitious in endless similarity.

Once more let the sun rise like today.
Did I say, "Once more"? No, indefinitely,
each time exactly the same as before,
no differentiation between first and last,
each dawn identical in time and space.

I want this noon to be like all noons,
dividing light in halves, marking before
and after, sitting midway in diurnal circles,
the morning history, a remembered past,
the afternoon promise, hastening, vast.

Let the hying sun go down heroically
in invincible retreat, in infinite encores,
shining substantial goodbyes to us all
in clear skies, a sharp light, a soft fall
that whispers truth about coming night.

Let every quotidian minute recur,
every tick of the clock tick on all over,
every hourly chime chiming, bell tolling,
cuckoo in the cuckoo clock cuckooing,
every tock of the clock intoning time.

Give me please this day always new,
a viable, vacant canvas still sublime,
twenty-four hours seamlessly flowing,
a slip of eternity's river, a dream-eddy
for experiencing the world and knowing.

Give it to me all blank to be written on
with indelible inks of blood and love,
a time never to be relegated to a shelf,
unending palimpsest, living never stayed,
malleable moments ever on parade.

World Inside

> *A light he was to no one but himself...*
> — Robert Frost

All outside of flesh is only ambience to consciousness,
mere flotsam and jetsam in the river of space/time:
here a father, there a lover, here a stranger, there a friend
as the river of space/time flows in eddies and cataracts
from its Big Bang beginning to its Apocalyptic end,
mountains, continents, oceans, and stars all colliding,
eliding, temporarily abiding together then gliding away
into disorder and dissolution for nothing, nothing can stay.

We are lights to ourselves alone, candles in our own dark,
and we guide ourselves deathward, our thoughts photons
that light our understanding of every lepton and quark
accompanying us on our flow along in currents of chaos,
this light the magic of imagination, the fire of dreams,
our consciousness itself an unquenchable metaphysical spark.

Great Misery Island, Salem Harbor, Massachusetts

With beers he stole from his father's stash,
with a broad blanket and his mother's car,
he took me to West Beach and we rowed across
summer water into an island's sandy nook,
an island long abandoned to shrubs and moss,
red maple and black cherry, white pine
and northern bay with its lavender berry.

We were alone, I being his, he being mine.
Sailboats surrounded the island, sunlight
glinting off white canvas sails, glistening
on sparse grass dew, gladdening day,
gleaming on tops of slight gray waves.
We knew we were watched from offshore,
a guy with binoculars focused on our play.

Paying no mind to a sailboat audience of one,
my boyfriend coaxed me out of my clothes,
took me into the water to sport with me, while
laughing gulls rose laughing, brown thrashers
posed thrashing, and I was splayed on the sand
for his pleasure, my body his fleshy treasure,
and our sailboat watcher cheered him on with
an airhorn— the only salute he had at hand.

Despite Robert Moulton's 1620s wailing
during an island landing here to wait out
a winter blow, his temperament quailing,
his food and water low, his sails furled,
from my own erotic experience, this is
the most misnamed island in the world!

Love in Time

One does the best one can, in politics, or in love.
One respects life, in oneself and in others.
One loves, and grows old. There is nothing to fear,
and nothing to care for, but love and time.
      —J. P. Seaton

Space/time, from its inception through to its demise,
contains within it all there is on this side of oblivion,
and should someone, somewhere, sometime devise
a method to peer beyond the physically detectable,
that person might be in for an apocalyptic surprise:
a metaphysical continuum exists, and love is its light,
and people who focus on the sensual certainly miss
realizing the ambience of eternal and infinite bliss.

Love is shot through space/time, surrounding it,
confounding it, elating its cataracts and eddies,
ablating, abrading sorrows massive and quantum,
for nothing is more permanent nor ethereal than
love, which keeps humanity from the damnation of
going through life believing the end is negation.

Koan

> *I have reached no conclusions, have erected no boundaries,*
> *shutting out and shutting in, separating inside*
> *from outside: I have*
> *drawn no lines . . .*
> — A. R. Ammons

I've walked below high-tide lines on childhood's beaches,
footprinted my bare feet in moist sand, my soft, bare soles
leaving behind flesh's eternal testament to impermanence.

The young-adult heart reaches for Eden's infinity,
believing ever-vernal love to be one of life's goals,
unaware the awaiting autumn's slow sever is so deceiving.

As an old man, I've learned what space-time teaches
about human intellect foundering on mortality's shoals,
and I've come to find my end both revealing and relieving.

What marks have I left? What marks by me will remain?
Certainly not words. Words last longest as poems
that retain the heftier parts of their creators' souls,

but they, too, disappear with our flimsy electronics,
our moldering books, our cloudy libraries of outdated
technologies and artificial brains of cracks and holes

where all old thoughts in Boolean logic go to die.
Words are fragile, fraught with error, ephemera
on the wing to nowhere, ultimately lost, unsought.

Not a line will outlast chaos, inhumane reality's
quantum physics overlapping metaphysics, our
mad religions grasping, grappling all for naught.

My voice will not outlive my passionless breath;
my kiss will not make tender a moment more
than my space-time's truncation made by death.

I am in contact with a Cosmos not knowing goodbye.
I am transitioning forever with stones and stars,
darkness and light, now beyond ever asking why.

My Boyfriend is an Asian Dragon

It is spring, kind of like spring, some form of spring
if not in the reality of my five senses, then in the reality
of my mind, and from the pristine depths of my desire,
or from the semi-polluted wellsprings of my desire,
or from the fetid swamp of my most secret desire,
change comes as he rises writhing in his smooth way
to hover over me, still wet from the water of my mouth,
my sweat, my eyes that widen at the sight of his snake-
like twisting torso, a visual, fleshy, artistic statement
that nothing will be the same and that I should prepare
for things to be different, his fingers lightning swift
to clasp parts of me I suddenly realize are mine but
over which I no longer have control, his mouth open
to take in parts of me I have to surrender, a lock of hair
spilling over his forehead to brush my face as he digs in
to enjoy whatever, and the ceiling is the sky, and my bed
the Planet Earth, and my house Heaven, the Universe,
all the galaxies gathering to watch him prey and feast,
the Horsehead Nebula frozen in its gazing at the scene
of me being taken naked into the Apocalypse of his
thrashing and lashing, his eel-like slithering over me,
on me, in me until even ritual and sanctity and dogma
and culture and bright red lines that cannot be crossed
are crossed, and he descends violently into my blood,
around my bones, throughout my mind until I cry out,
"Yes! Thank God for this! Thank God I'm mortal!
I thank God, eaten alive, devoured along the Way!"

Stardust

But that was long ago, and now my consolation
is in the stardust of a song.
    — Mitchell Parish

What were they, those days both blue and gold?
When were they, Sodom and Gomorrah of our own
making? Nothing stays. All floats and flows
out of our orbit, circling us a while until we're old
and we watch as what once was splendor goes.
We, adrift in our present circumstance, remember
brightness before our past froze into place, love left,
and age and illness have us bereft of time and space.

We will love again beyond reason, beyond rhyme,
again in our hour of roistering mortality— that is to say,
in imaginative recollection and uninhibited by time,
the dust of all of us having settled, the dust star-deep
blotting out everything human, but not the sublime
that is our ageless consciousness forever in its prime.

Coronavirus

*To believe that our beliefs
are permanent truths which encompass reality
is a sad arrogance.*
  — Ursula K. Le Guin

Little darling daring to rule the planet,
you are doing to us what we do to Earth—
you, an infectious insurrection cleansing,
in a way, a world made sick by people.

See where rivers made rotten by human
ingenuity come clean as you prick cells
to reproduce yourselves and Earth breathes
more freely as our own morbidity swells.

Nature invented you to clean house,
repairing damage we've done to a planet
that didn't deserve human-caused sickness,
nature wisely inventing you to kill a louse.

Already with some thousands of us dead
and the rest stilled by fear, the good Earth
is recovering from human infection instead
of succumbing to "civilization's" spread.

You are a planet's medicinal response
to a fearsome despoiler and destroyer
that pollutes and plunders with a nonchalance
that chills as it does what blindly it wills,

and while humans think of you unkindly,
nature loves you, knows you to be a hero
in eternal battles for life's survival, taking,
if necessary, the number of humans to zero.

Ambient Air

> *Is that a song, under the shouting?*
> — Kim Stafford

Human doubting, flouting, outing, pouting, routing,
scouting, spouting, sprouting, and touting are noises
that mask heartbeat rhythms that love employs
lying meekly under civilization's bleak shouting,
quiet sounds, they are, having a semblance of song.

Lilac lyrics lie languishing in long-forgotten gardens
of one's childhood where youth played soprano
to space/time's ever undulating bass, for age hardens
the understanding of what once was clear rhythm
and rhyme, like childhood disappearing without a trace.

Even a tambourine rustle of oak leaves in winter wind
is drowned out by highway traffic, workday bustle,
daily hustle to get minutiae done, the feisty vying of
pride with desire overpowering life's softer chorales
lying hidden under dubious duties of culture's prison.

Animal arias rise from both vernal and autumnal woods,
everything from thrushes to cougars in choir to nature,
knowing as they do how fleet of foot is life, how brief
anguish, how impermanent and unimportant grief,
how vastly symphonic and operatic life's orgiastic cry.

Never ask what lies beneath common noise of a day,
a week, a month, a year, for all surfaces are transitory,
all surfaces surfeiting with their common blandness,
while oratorios for blood and bone rise from under
space/time's superficialities, the wise hearing their tone.

Put the din in the distance and ride away on a song
that has infinity as its theme, its libretto on eternity,
and know the distractions of the flesh are not for long,
nor are the palpitations of a workday, sighs or sorrow,
for the song you hear under the shouting is tomorrow.

May You Live in Interesting Times

> *May you live in interesting times.*
> — Ancient Chinese Curse

And may you be granted a long life ensconced
in human ego's lust after wealth and power,
granted illusions drawn by your five senses,
granted dust of ten thousand things you think
you possess in the darkness before dawn,
granted delusions of material grandeur that link
success to wealth and physical strength, war
and conquest, flesh your plaything and pawn.

And may you, at some inappropriate time, love.
May the dust of your own making hide you
from reality and the interminable flow of rivers
upon which ten thousand things go, you, believing,
trusting, mussing, rusting, fussing as you come to
light your way with memory's diminishing glow.

Dust Mites

Living in dust, thriving in dust, creating dust,
our bodies, our skin incessantly flaking it off,
we accompany clouds of dust in our minds with
crowds of dust stirred with a sneeze, a cough
as we move indecently through ambient air
that would be cleaner, fresher were we not there.

At night, lying awake in any bed of our making,
or lying asleep in the steam of illicit dreaming,
or tossing, turning in the tussle of our partaking
in love-making and body-sharing, we shed dust
of ourselves everywhere in the room's dark,
ourselves a source of detritus: our skin's crust.

Add to human flotsam and jetsam on life's river
accumulating waste of the mind's false beliefs
and we have the makings of intellectual entropy
with no more creative power than that of a ghost,
mental saprophytism devolving into parasitism,
an evolving entity eventually harming its host.

Ignore them, the tiny creatures feeding off what drops
from us, what we shed, almost invisible scraps
of ourselves we leave lying behind ourselves,
our consciousness moving on, ourselves not unlike
dust mites feeding, vying, breeding, dying for
sustenance before their share of space/time is gone.

... They Moved Together Through Dust and Dragons ...

When we began loving each other, we were naïve, glad
of ignorance, our innocence, and our absence of wisdom
that would come later in a heat in a hurry. What we had
was space/time in which to ride away in lives replete
with happenstance and accident, chaos and imagination.

Culture kicked up dust, threw it in our faces, in our eyes:
adult fairytales of deities, survival instincts gone wild,
bigotries ingrained in childhood, sophistries and lies,
dust that hides reason, dust that floats on ego's tides,
dust we learned to brush away season after season.

And dust ourselves off we did, dusting off each other
in each other's arms, in each other's dreams, aware
as we were that what matters is beyond confections
cooked up by our five senses, that what matters lies
safely in oblivion beyond space/time's infections.

What matters is voiced in the silence of held hands,
two bodies in bed holding each other night-long,
guarding a union of two consciousnesses before
they unite again in eternity's supreme togetherness,
all things of yore uniting in absence's undying song.

As we floated fondly together away from and toward
nothingness (that is, away from birth toward death),
what worlds did we create, puzzles solve, rivers ford
on our way hither, thither, and yon on a narrow way
that broadens as metaphysical understandings evolve?

And there were dragons. And they were very real.
They rose of their own accord to lord chaotically
over catastrophe, apocalypse, bringing to human fates
violent change, opportunities dragons arrange only for
those deemed worthy of prevailing in altered states.

And we loved each other in spite of human follies,
through bodily pains and mental anguish, in spite of
tricks and sabotage aging plays on the engaging mind;
in defiance of space/time's distractions and in lieu of
the acceptance of evil, we gave to love all our reliance.

Beatitude 1

Blessed are the poor in spirit,
for theirs is the Kingdom of Heaven.

But I could've loved you, would've, too.
I'd have been true and then some.
I'm no fool, knowing as we both know
the Kingdom of Heaven resides
uninhibited between your thighs
where you work your thralldom,
your lips' delicious mucus membrane,
your thickening voice, your dilated eyes,
your orgasm shouted out like anger . . .

But I watch the Kingdom of Heaven fade
afterward when you're done and satisfied
and I'm not, and I watch you in all your
languor and liquids love leaves behind
after love's over and played itself out,
after your anatomically correct passion dies
and you reach for clothes and car keys.
Unwise as always, I face that other side
of you that I could never please,
your orgasm having left us strangers . . .

But I could love you even then,
watching your heat freeze,
your lust turn to ennui and snow,
our marijuana high changing to headache,
my entreaties marking your time to go
with your sweet sweat gone clammy
and my purple moment torn asunder,
your orgasm left inside me like woe . . .

But I could love you even then,
you staring at me that cold way
wondering how poorly I might behave,
desperate at our final break. Stay,
Kingdom of Heaven! Poor in spirit,
I see you sulk away in orgasm's sullen wake.

Beatitude 2

Blessed are those who mourn,
for they shall be comforted.

Love plies like life plies, languidly, a day at a time.
Lust-struck youth goes beachcombing through
bright morning, becoming "old folks" slowly,
long in a gloaming that lies between realization
and remembrance, cooling pubescent pleasure's
warm saliva into cold, senescent drool.

Senility's not-so-subtle weltering puts us here
in our pool's shallow end where we stub toes,
stumble and thrash, looking back wistfully
to the long-ago deep end where we still see
blissful youngsters' pleasurable splash.

But love knows no such horseplay's rigor mortis.
Unbenumbed by age, love will never go away,
abiding as sharply at eighty as at eighteen,
an aching beyond where even mourning dies.

Still here? Love, fumbling with this and that
among the brain's last bric-a-brac, still causes
a caught breath even as the body fills our agenda
with task-canceling, calendar-clearing death.

Late, isn't it? Love, shouldn't you be going?
Love, shouldn't you be gone? How strange love,
old and broken, shadow of what once was,
though deranged like life, steadfastly lingers on.

Beatitude 3

Blessed are the meek,
for they shall inherit the earth.

I look away— down, in fact, in submission to you,
your flesh ruling me like your stare, your bold
domination making me glad I am what I am, aware
of who I am and for what slim, fancy purpose you,
the God of Love, make the act of mating prayer.

I bow down before your energetic torso rising,
beneath your haughty eyes, my knees on the floor,
my fingers stroking your thick, young luck as I,
leaning back, passive to everything you want done,
part my lips to accept your muscular tongue.

I lie supine to your prone domination, eager
catcher to your pitcher, reveling in fever
of life between your thighs, beneath your hips,
your glands, the thrusts of your focused mind
binding me to you with slick, wet demands.

I offer you my flesh freely and am joy itself
in your fierce acceptance. I am fruitful in Eden
where you, God of Love, planted me, a crop
for your body to harvest in your full power,
riding me with a glide I never want to stop.

Back, forth, up, down, while I say new rosaries,
pray to hear your voice, my master, your sweat
a liquid where resistance drowns, my purpose
finding birth. Meek I am, dear God of Love,
and in your coming only, I inherit the earth.

Beatitude 4

*Blessed are those who hunger and thirst after righteousness,
for they shall be filled.*

So what do I do, I who hunger, thirst? I watch you,
my surreptitious eyes looking side-long, reaching askance
through the mind's uncloaking night, its license-giving dark,
baring, too, my character for an autonomic sexual shiver,
your fleshy shimmer becoming my summer's song,
fresh eye candy for everyday hungering and thirsting.

I watch you, but how? Unseen from too far afar, I catch
your muscular flex, view your rolling, liquid glide
on the nubile balls of your feet, your supple ride
on your hips through days where I remain unsuspected,
a feigned innocence rubbing my life's cycle against yours.
Undetected, I ply fearless, feckless far from civilizing norms
and sing a cappella silently inside your life, you unawake,
unaware of my delirious starvation, my dehydration
slakeable only by the liberties I'd take in your bed,
over and over seriously, over and over into ad nauseam
without mercy or regard for the living or dead.

Poem, psalm will be done when hunger lies slain,
thirst quenched: wanton, both of us together,
wet with sated love. Don't call it temptation.
The God of Love knows better. The table of life
is spread before us and we have only to wake
to eat each other's love, drink each other's love,
and become full of love for righteousness' sake.

Beatitude 5

Blessed are the merciful,
for they shall obtain mercy.

It won't always be now, there coming a time
when wine will not pour, gardens bloom, or birds sing
defending the infinite territories of their love.
It won't be now again, now when love awaits,
however quaint or silly or masochistically inclined,
when you see opportunity to slake another's thirst
for lust with fluid satisfactions you withhold as if
they were liquid gold. Another begs for you
and all Earth waits to see if you reply with dogma,
sophistry, or the insanely human heart. It won't be
the same as it's always been whether you make love
or not, never again such chances for enjoying mercy
delivered flesh to flesh meriting a god's applause.

All too soon it won't be now ever again, regardless
of flinty, catechistic truth, regardless of the world
as you think it should be, regardless of penance
for what you presumed to be sin and then some.
All too soon it will be time. And with its ending,
whether in paroxysm or asleep, in states of grace
or denial, whether silly little rights or wrongs
dominate the last ticking seconds of your existence,
you'll be gasping perhaps for breath, for release
of pain, for mercy, mercy, in the throes of death.

Then think of what love you've given mercifully
to those who've begged for your limbs and torso,
mind and body, pump and rub and thrill
spilling suddenly out and all over themselves.
Then think of love's mercy as you lie shocked
by life's lights flickering out within your eyes
and cancellation marks mar their way across
your suddenly vacuous skies, your vestigial
world a fast-receding waste, a new deep blank,
death now riding you in bed, riding roughshod,
you hoping in this unseemly onset of oblivion
your act of love endears you to a merciful God.

Beatitude 6

> *Blessed are the pure in heart,*
> *for they shall see God.*

I love innocently when I can, guiltily when I can't,
inappropriately, disproportionately, French kissing
so deeply my tongue moves past your gag reflex
to lick your larynx, sucking your splendor right out
of your mouth, swallowing your liquid satisfaction
that gods have envied as love's slaking liqueur.
When love's forbidden, then love in hiding,
love with little iniquities attached like spice.
Enter Eden tantalized, then sated. Humans teach
love beyond logic, no boundary, minus rules.
Scandalizingly love whoever comes within reach.

For instance, make do wrestling me in the buff,
me pinned again and again, through and through
pure in heart, thrashing about recklessly regretless,
afterward needing a wash, soap for our hands,
shampoo for our hair, rubs to relax our muscles,
replacement hormones for our overtaxed glands.
After a love and release, a heart's always pure.

Love with no holds barred wherever you are,
even here with me. See? Look at you even now
as I fumble with your buttons, zippers, Velcro
and snaps and stays torn open, undressing you,
sure and aroused. Amazed, stare as I play.
Let us bless while panting this physical bounty
of which we are about to partake, hearts pure
as the last naïve practitioners of love left awake.

Look, this isn't rocket science. Let us prepare
for worship by locking front doors, securing
that bedroom latch, letting down moral bars,
loving anyone, anyplace. There's no catch
for the pure in heart. Come here and feel,
in wetting bliss, the God of Love face to face.

Beatitude 7

> *Blessed are the peacemakers,*
> *for they shall be called sons of God.*

I let you go. Take love away from where I lie
newly reclusive, from where I alone will fight out
the last of love by crying, by losing memory,
my skin forgetting your touch, my mouth your taste,
my ears your tenor, my nose your sensual smell,
my eyes the darling heaven of your face.

I love you, so I make my peace with ache,
accept some agony as the price for living your lie.
I love you so I can't hold you. I can't harm you.
I chide my shriveled ego for wanting to fight unfair,
rising as I do above longing to shred your flesh
so none will want you, have you, love you.

And now it's starting, my recovery from our affair,
as I keep the peace and let you off smiling, deceived;
I, smiling, backing down from nastiness so colossal
awe-struck neighbors would jostle crime scene tape
to wonder at ruination and arrest of me, the bereaved.

Let's let it be. I love you more than enough to suffer
humility, humbled even as you pack and tell me
she has this or that virtue, in this or that moment
she caught your heart. I know, I think, how God felt
with callow Adam bored in Eden, God aggrieved,
God willing for His love of Adam to create an Eve.
I know why we laud those who keep the peace,
those lonely sons of God.

Beatitude 8

*Blessed are those who are persecuted for righteousness' sake,
for theirs is the kingdom of heaven.*

Lovers (and who are more persecuted than they?)
are righteous, punished for their pleasure and promise
in chastity's dark ages, persecuted for a lusty heart
where dogma casts no shadow, where altar candelabra
cannot drizzle flesh minus clothing with hot wax dicta
fomenting fulminating disgrace, where no sizzling griddles
of religious doctrine await those in bliss who get supine
beneath bodies prone. Lovers alone and unextolled
do the God of Love's heavy-lifting, do it with muscle,
correctly. Lovers' sweat lubricates law, lightens life
in an orgasmic hustle, ejecting every human flaw.

Love, even when forbidden, abides. Love persecuted
finds ways to thrive. Ask gays, ask boys and girls
and Walt Whitman. Ask yourself. Sweet, slick moistures
bodies make are thank-yous, encouragement to continue,
rewards for persevering. Slippery moistures from the mouth
and elsewhere are the terrain of the Kingdom of Heaven,
though loveless angels lacking requisite skill and equipment
are appalled, tsk-tsking along Heaven's golden roads
as spent lovers enter two-by-two beguiling even Peter who,
if the truth be known, passes them on smiling. Lovers need
not worry nor crawl on hands and knees before envious
angels. Copulating is righteousness stripped to essentials,
leavening thickly a Kingdom of Heaven newly theirs.

I, Dragon

I too am not a bit tamed, I too am untranslatable.
I sound my barbaric yawp over the roofs of the world.
   — Walt Whitman

I, too, do not know from where I came. I hover shivering,
shimmering, smooth, and slippery above terrain I was given.
I float before my lover, glimmering in his eyes, and I realize
in that moment I perform infinitesimally small miracles,
illimitable numbers of them in his blood, in his brain.
I am his earth, ocean, everything worthwhile under his skies,
and although momentarily aroused or momentarily sated,
he is afraid of my power to be what I am, power to leave him,
his hour with my body, on my body, in my body both ecstasy
and terror. I twist and slither this way and that under him,
over him, and naked; I hang in air above his consciousness,
and I am in control of fantastic realities, realistic fantasies,
and nothing can console him for having been born to desire,
for helplessly rewarding himself with blushing capitulation
to copulation, thus coming awake to his own natural fire.

I sound my sybaritic tenor cry over the proofs of science
and culture and religion that deny my existence, but I am.
Those who've seen and felt my flesh do not deny change
ensues when I rise, chaos has come, chaos that has potential
for flesh's effulgence, love in futurity, lust in the present,
chaos that is merely infinite change, opportunities everywhere,
for a consciousness that understands space/time demands
and nakedly invites the twists, flips, and slithers, matter
and anti-matter, ecstasies that flow from another's hands
that knead and need me, that plead with me and flatter
me with promises unable to be kept, the dragon of me

suddenly writhing seductively, instructively, ineluctably
in my unwound body, my unbound mind tossing off
dogma to explicate for my lover the untranslatable text
of change; I, dragon, readying him for all coming next.

Disbelief

But one by one my friends fell away from our reality's beauty, their senses aged and overcome, their minds in disheveling dust, their futures reduced to life's gloamings, their sour experiences leveling their dreams, their imaginations now coated with rust.

And so it is that though song sparrows call and larks respond, they hear none of lilt and laughter, busy with daily artificialities, dizzy with dogma and dicta, not aware that dawn has dawned, its sun-streamed lightness enveloping all that night has spawned.

They have become zombies. They slow-walk their bodies through mindless routines learned rotely, slowly and somewhat irresolutely stomping forward through the day's weeds as stomp they must, throwing up their arms, growing alarmed as in gods they trust.

What once they were, they are no more, not even lesser shadows of truth, shrouds covering what they once dreamed, nor are they receptive to sustenance of clouds, rivers, and mountains theirs for the taking if they could empty their hearts and minds of clay.

What once they were was beautiful. What once they were sang like clouds, rivers, and mountains sing the clear and ringing song of consciousness yearning with a heart, of consciousness awake and aware and burning to turn even the wrong and the fake to art.

As children, they and I floated on the flow of space/time along with all else, knowing as only children know, wise as one can be only before everything succumbs chaotically to our five senses and we mistake sparks for stars and piddling noise for symphony.

As adolescents, they and I parted company to pursue rectitude
and frivolity, they choosing the practical, the sensible, the sane,
while I elected erotica surreptitiously becoming ambience, love
buoying me up as I employed, enjoyed life on a different plane.

Who was happier? Who was right? May I silently suggest
it was I. Embracing metaphysics as it has never been embraced,
I even now ride high over youth's ashes, my consciousness
unimperiled by five senses on my eternal and infinite quest.

My friends, they fluster in stress, flounder in dust, falsify joy,
and do not in their stifling mortality see how five senses deceive,
and truly bereft of awareness of their transience in space/time,
they do not believe. They do not believe. They do not believe.

COVID-19

And so snow-like dust, settled on the frozen lake of human ambition, explodes in late winter's wrath of another dragon's awakening, dust scattered, ice shattered, reality splattered with human attrition caused by a dragon in the form of a virus splashing change about, a dragon slashing change that gives human complacency the rout, and we and all things react, some destroyed, some buoyed, some, even in the heft of their despondency, suddenly renewed to a life awake and aware of opportunity that indifferently leaves others bereft.

Thanks to the dragon, apocalypse has come to what wealthy see as Eden. To what the poor see as Pandemonium. To what religions see as Sodom and Gomorrah. To what the awake and aware see as this world's lung-clogging, mind-boggling dust arises, flies free, blinds and binds: a virus this time, a virus inept and ill-equipped to harm consciousness floating, flowing, loving serendipitously.

Consciousness on the Way

The mind is a sense organ and objects are its sensations . . .
Forget the mind and objects; it's your nature that is real.
— Yung-chia

I recreate my history more to my liking, the way
historians see events as they weren't, debate issues
that were undebated, making those who never spoke
have a say, giving voice to thoughts left unsaid,
reading between lines what writers wished unread;
in short, fictionalizing facts, factualizing fiction,
neatly trimming, skimming acts, adding, padding,
simplifying, complicating: every historian's addiction.

I do this to myself because I'm out of my mind
literally. I am a consciousness, awake and aware
of my ephemeral body's slogging through space/time,
my prying mind preoccupied with my five senses trying
to give sensations interpretations, reason and rhyme,
I, a consciousness apart, participating in birthing, dying.

My Grandmother Busies Herself in My Kitchen

> *I believe home reflects the spirit of the homemaker.*
> — Betty Crocker

Holiday's here again, and again I won't cook.
I don't cook, and my immaculate, state of the art,
high-end kitchen shows it. Intricate, random patterns
of brown-gold granite stretch with a glossy sheen
beneath oak cabinets, around an inset gas range,
above high-tech double ovens, countertops agleam,
spanking-new butcher block ready for fancy cutting,
computer-tamed appliances winking their lights
back at my chef stove's bright-faced timer clock.

You'd think a woman as old as she would be lost
among modern kitchen gadgetry, today's cooking
more calculated chemistry, artistry computer-tossed,
than old-fashioned fare served heartily, abundantly,
a cornucopia offered all with grandmotherly flair
and the result of days of preparation, anticipation,
hours of stewing and brewing busy with laughter.
But she's here. She's aware. She's watching
somewhere from the eleventh quantum dimension

as her grandson prepares on this night to eat alone,
her hands softer, perhaps, than they were a while ago
but nevertheless still reassuringly on my shoulders,
their pressure ever and always an easy one to feel,
her voice as clear as the day she first said my name,
her arms inclusive of everyone in need of a meal.
Her eyes still can't take in enough of me to satisfy
her nagging fear that she might disappear before
she's shown me how food can be a language of love.

She's speaking only to me in my empty kitchen,
telling me again down decades that fell away fast,
across gulfs unbridgeable except by fond ghosts,
over humdrum and stolid days of no importance,
that what's essential is inside the mind and body,
what's filling and fulfilling should be love's labor
laboring on, being illuminated by the mind's eye,
meals shared preternaturally with loves here or gone,
bread broken over separations, hopes fed unspoken.

There Be Dragons

They lie awakening at the bottom of still waters,
ready to be rancorous and writhing, rising high
to the pond, lake, river, ocean surface where
they will fly explosively into space/time and air,
storm-glad and splashing brouhahas over order
until foaming is assured, apocalyptic froth nigh,
Chinese dragons fomenting, forming the Way,
heaven leavened with their awry, slithering play.

Indifferent to humans, they've their own business
to attend, but in their swirls and curls, wriggles
and wiggles, grasps and gasps, they conjure storm
and create change, opportunities for those worthy:
those who float on rivers and wander mountains,
those who do not find this pregnant chaos strange.

Simplification

In simplicity, I nurture Way my own way.
In quiet mystery, things seen are thoughts felt.
  — Tu Fu

How simple can I get? Jettisoning experiences right and left,
abandoning aging, letting go of life's lessons both swift and deft,

I lie alert, allowing a garden sun to warm my hardened face,
to shine light on my new innocence, my new simplicity a grace.

I nurture and am nurtured, know and am known, learn
    and am learned;
feeling my way from and to oblivion is a way
    both given and earned.

It's a quiet mystery how in my mind's eye I remain a boy at play:
cool, callow, pure if shallow, sensing only consciousness can stay.

Only my insentient thoughts are felt. Only invisible thoughts
    are seen.
Only my imagined thoughts are real. From my thoughts I glean

the tenuous union of the physical with the metaphysical, feel
the powers of consciousness and oblivion and how they heal.

The river of space/time flows chaotically yet methodically on,
its cataracts and eddies eternally coming, going, dusk to dawn

while I, in my raw simplicity, find my place in love and wine,
in soft acceptance of change, the awe of it all ultimately mine.

I Am Who I Am

Wind is unaware of who I am. Unknown am I
to the unwitting grass, and to the diffident sunlight
I am less known than the unremitting night, I,
who still has eternity to pass, though not in a form
I wear now. I am anonymous to the amorphous sea,
unidentifiable to cumulonimbus clouds that storm
arbitrarily over space-time, and unremembered by
clothes and toys and ghosts that I once held dear.

Undaunted by exclusions, elisions, eliminations
that forsake my name, I go to oblivion without fear,
I, a stream of vibrations briefly me, a consciousness
perceiving itself to be, I, leaving nothing of myself,
a shadow's shadow in a sublime sweep, a whisper
of a wisp without grief, but with infinity to reap.

Why the Night Sky Is Dark

In an infinite universe, stars would be visible everywhere and their collective light would be so intense that night would be brighter than day. But the light from far stars has not had time to reach us, indicating that the universe is not infinite, is not old, but is in fact young. Very young.
— Professor Alex Filippenko
University of California, Berkeley

Stars all unthought of, let alone unseen,
sling out photons pell-mell toward us,
light racing light years toward us in our
uncentered place in a young universe
where we await sudden appearances of
trillions of heretofore unknown new stars
in stunning brightnesses turning night sky
into light, an awesome luminescence like
the surface of the sun, white-hot, afire.

Cool! Very young is our Cosmos' desire,
globs of innocence clinging arousingly
to its luminous flesh flung hotly across
expansion to be sucked on and devoured
by black holes of lust and experience.

Blasted into being a few short billion
ago when the greatest orgasm known
to envious man spilled from a **Big Bang**
over everything waiting and watching;
the universe has come so alive, sexy
as only the truly young can be sexy,
smoking hot as only the truly cute

can be smoking hot, wet as only love
can really know what wetness means,
the universe impresses in its teens:
savage beauty of youth, infectious will,
adolescent refusal to obey any orders
of adults jaded by their last cheap thrill.

Milky Way

> *The wiggly lines on the bottom of the bars*
> *come from the belt they ride on while cooling.*
> — Milky Way Brand Website

The wiggly lines twirl stupendously
slowly in their evolutionary burning
through the universe's chocolate night
on a journey from creation to oblivion,
the wiggly lines bright bars on a belt
that circles a dark center unlit by stars.

The wiggly lines are a bottom of reality
arcing in its strenuous, tenuous turning,
a hundred billion suns rotating around
and exalting a black hole's thick nougat
of egg-white light whipped into a frappe,
time and space a frothed cocoa malt.

In the soft, sugared lark of childhood,
in the cocoa-butter sweet of childhood,
how the universe tastes scrumptious,
frosted galaxies honeyed and neat,
love's first possibilities coming storied
in a candied Cosmos, a sensual treat.

Orbis Non Sufficit

Even this winter dies. Even blank, clammy January
eventually finds sleep in February's slightly lighter skies,
February itself yielding dank, cold ground to wet March,
though while caught in my own year's old-age ill-humor,
future times that hint of spring bliss appear to be fantasy,
and a coming of April's afterlife is, for me, only rumor.

I'm too old for this. I'm alone. I busy myself poorly
among my yesterday's fond bric-a-brac, paper and ink
too ephemeral, my wan thoughts too ethereal to atone
for all else I've had fall away; I think my days of
caper and laughter lie ghostly behind me, my creativity
slain, my curiosity drained, aged, killed, blood and bone.

My gait is a shuffle, my leaps relegated to imagination,
my once-lively step stilled. And to what end do I wait?
What's left to be gained? I have turned to stone. See?
My fate no longer involves practice of flesh's luxuries,
nor does it open toward uncharted, unpredictable roads
of youth, fulfillment. Elderly delirium has a date with me.

How can a man in his end time, his dotage, be guilty
of anything mildly akin to sin? And yet, and yet . . .
As my flesh rejects this world, my mind wildly conjures
heavens and hells apropos to judgment, grief, and regret.
My heart, loving to no avail, worn down, worn out,
would rather fail and sleep than to suffer a new start.

I've not learned enough to make me crave immortality.
I've lived, done my time, occupied my space, earned
whatever spiritual recompense experience provides
to the human race for chaos, pain, and indifference
of the universe that together require us to invent gods
and their adolescent behavior to keep ourselves sane.

I am so far past redemption, reinvention, reincarnation
that I've come to accept Oblivion's benevolence, pray
for nothing beyond the grave save the purity of demise.
Give me nothing but dust and non-existence's salvation.
The world is not enough. I would have solitude's solace,
knowing now how embracing earthly loss makes us wise.

A Dragon Speaks

Is it cancer, death, lost love, divorce, poverty?
Is it change, change that hurts you so, blights
that rearrange your life, your thin philosophies
that find a violation of their tenants so strange
that you switch gods and dogma hunting for
annihilation of pain in different religious rites?

Look! I grasp in my claws a pearl, world, sun,
what have you, and I snarl as I swirl and let fly
change you fear, and I force ties to be undone,
trusts to break, give the lie to plans and bans
and the worth of material wealth however won
as an altogether different opportunity expands.

A death? A change to travel on your own
in the flow of space/time, learning each life
is alone, each consciousness a product of seeds
metaphysically sown, each life responsible
for seeing to its own needs, each traveler along
space/time singular, solitary, blood and bone.

A cancer? A change to assess and weigh
the worth of your flesh in the scheme of things
and the birth of a new world view, a fresh take
on the value of each new day as an opportunity
to learn wisdom, to recognize the true, to make
yourself a part of the artful, ever-flowing Way.

A lost love? A change to say a final goodbye
to a baleful vanity that entrapped you a while,
the thought that you are master of attachments,
controller of another soul, and now you smile
to know the truth that passion is flesh's guile
better left alone if enlightenment is your goal.

A divorce? A change of weather, that's all.
A change that opens opportunities for going on
into the blue haply alone, having grown tall
in experience and self-salvation, having thrown
caution to the winds in favor of a new dawn
to a day seeing you freshened, tint and tone.

Poverty of what? Of spirit? Of hope? Poverty
is like chastity: overcome with common sense
and gumption and knowing that fulfillment
is becoming oneself part of the world's wealth,
the physical world's treasures being immense,
the wise using change as a part of self-defense.

When I am aroused, energized, on the loose,
I convolute human reality, plans, space/time.
I am change only a philosopher understands.
I bring violent perspective to physicality's void.
I wake those hands who know this seminal truth:
The only wasted life is the life not enjoyed.

Adagio for Alpenhorns

When a noble life has prepared for old age,
it is not decline that it reveals,
but the first days of immortality.
    — Madame de Stael

Early morning, and this past spring's fawns champ grass
on a pre-winter wold that slants heavily away toward
human-inhabited valleys below where lights blink out
at the coming of dawn. Deer have autumn days to pass
fattening, following the base of each mountain fold,
while I think of saving myself now that summer's gone,
and I see sunlight whiten snow high up above me,
brighten tops of mountains, light slowly seeping down
to turn gray-blue snow to sharp white. Standing here,
feet braced on a steep decline, I watch pine siskins dot
and dash among cones of fir, hemlock, cedar, and spruce,
yellow slashes on brown-streaked wings flicking against
green swags of needles, little brown things that twitter
and wheeze soft cheeps as they peck seeds, then flicker,
flitter around and about branches in feathery throes
to tease each other as if no oncoming cold mattered,
as if a prime fall day would ever please, never close.

They're coming awake in villages scattered below,
some few, I'm sure, looking out of their windows to see
bright white of snow-capped summits, light moving down
in slow progression to cause upland meadows to glow
and glisten high above them, after which they return
to whatever possesses them and their day. They won't
see me, nor will they listen for siskins, feel ice's burn
on the face, the hands, on anything bared to the weather

at this altitude well on the way to winter before the valleys
know. People down there on their little ribbons of road
go back and forth, threading their asphalt way here and there,
searching for stuff in which they think happiness abides,
fleeing dismay, avoiding getting off track and spinning
wheels in composting floors of forest duff; people unaware
of death's translucence, people thinking death opaque,
people never surmising mortality's only time and space,
after which history sleeps and imagination comes awake.

Autumn-bound (that is, bound by autumn), I'm as far
from village life as any villager has the means to be,
leaving behind parks and perks and community privilege,
getting of things, avoiding of things, fretting not being free,
letting myself imprison myself with cares wrapped like
chit-chat around conversations I'd rather not have had. I,
autumn-bound, am readjusting my sights to the icy scree
above the tree line that leaves off where the living depart
and the terrain, forever snow-blasted, rises steeply in sharp air,
giving me fodder for rumination and threats to take to heart.
From here on, I'll be having a conversation with myself
about what it means to be human and what it meant to be me.
From here on, I'll be undergoing a conversion from seducer
and succorer to seed, my fleshy diminution and devolution
not demeaning me, but leaving me more in thought than deed,
finally realizing I won't have answers to mystery, don't have
to know, don't have a claim to thorns or roses, don't need.

I have used my body to form my mind, to inform my soul.
I've been educated by hormones and endorphins, chastised
by pain, brought to understanding even against my will
by working life's meter and rhyme into thought, by finding
in the damnedest places footprints of old loves from before.
If space/time is a wall between me and immortality, death

is its door. Imagination is a keyhole. I put my eye to it
and see blurrily what's in store after my last breath, my eye
not being my mind's eye which focuses much more clearly
through human civilization that otherwise blinds, and I know
instinctively to trust subatomic particles, dark energy, dark
matter to lead me off mountains, out of valleys. Ultimately
what the heart searches for, the spirit finds. Ultimately
autumn becomes spring, hills become dales, flesh becomes
dreams as death will bring to reality that awe hope streams.
I have used my mind to form the world. I've been educated
by angels and demons who've kept my eternity undefined.

Hallelujahs and amens ring autumnally over slopes and fields
where snowfields are surely to come, lauds and prayers pass
from vale to vale in fall breezes, while the deer here moments ago
have gone, sunlight finally reaching that part of autumn morning
where I stand unseen by waking villagers stirring stolidly below,
though they be looking out of windows right at the hillside where
winter will be soon enough, where before long no one will come.
They see me not with eyes not used for seeing, feel with senses
not used for feeling, numbed by incessant daily living to a point
where fear replaces magic, gripping replaces giving, the soul
tenses at the cold suggestion of ending, and they cannot know,
cannot show, cannot go. At best, they hope for serendipity to
make things right, and I love them every one, blowing them a kiss
from my distance from them, throwing them a kiss from my
departure among mountains as I move along, the low music
of my heartbeat echoing above far valleys letting me know,
if unconsciously, each vibration is a note of immortality's song.

Hear it? Or is it always beyond the human ear? Beyond your
detection in a muddle of daily living, so much noise to interfere
with deep-cord inflection rising, falling, waxing, waning, distant
always but there. Move more upland or sally down to any hollow

between mountains and you'll not be lost to its haunting call
so like a tone set at the start of the Big Bang, a background moan
that grows clearer when trees lose their sere leaves in the fall
and the sound reverberates as an ambience to your work or play
out here in the high country of your closing day. "It's all right,"
it means. "You'll be safe. Come home," and the tone abides
even after dusk, even after forgetfulness robs your brain of care,
even after pain dissolves reason, even after you've become alone
as the tides of dissolution are awash in your flesh in the season
of your leaving blood and bone behind, as you wend your way
out of the Solar System and onto what you once thought oblivion
which, at the last moment, you come to understand is immortality,
singing what is ever a love song, finally taking you by the hand.

Eternity's love song echoes from slope to slope, and echoes on
into the heavens, reverberating off subatomic particles, entering
consciousness photon by photon, neutrino by neutrino, telling us
we have always been. We will always be. We are genetically
programmed to contribute ourselves to immortality. Look where
the sunlight reaches the valley bottom, brightening even asphalt
roads and ramshackle homes, where its vibration teaches us
not to fear autumn but to ride out space and time, to hold hands,
to imagine infinity wrapped tightly within us, not to fear autumn
but to abide our fleshy span with a nod toward the sublimity
of existing forever. Hear the bass note vibrating in the heart
of every atom, rebounding off the background radiation of the
universe, existence's deep notes underscoring our soprano song,
ourselves a moment of movement, a briefer than Planck time
vibration tossed among pines and firs and mountain meadows
and glistening peaks, bass notes to accompany our walk across
Eden, in winter on our way out of and into yet another sublime.

Centripetal Versus Centrifugal

These forces are part of the flow of space/time,
tugging inextricably, inexplicably, inexorably
on me as my consciousness courses through
cataracts and chasms, life's throes and spasms,
outward from oblivion, inward toward apocalypse.

I am drawn downward by dust's universal gravity,
falling inward toward the strong center of myself
from which all qualities emerge: rectitude, depravity,
lust, chastity, every ablative desire, every creative urge
that makes me human to imagine, to learn, to aspire.

The centripetal pull is enormous. It will not let go.
I face the central core from where I came and yearn,
in spite of blinding dust, for all I knew and loved of yore,
in spite of binding cultures that would hold me longer,
and their force is remembrance leaving me wanting more.

I am drawn outward by dragons of change that lure me,
rising into mental machinations unachievable in space/time,
my mind taught, fraught, brought by imagination's magic
to a realization of my consciousness floating on the flow
of all things toward an end seen either as resolving or tragic.

The centrifugal pull is enormous. It will not let go.
I erase my past as I lean into its power, dust of this world
blown away by the flashes of change from the lashes
of a dragon's tail, and clean, clear, empty I rise newly
oblivious to space/time's deceit, trusting dreams prevail.

And so I flow through space/time both attaching to you
and detaching, pulled to you, pulled away from you,
propelled, impelled, and expelled; your body attracting,
your mind impacting my satellite life's circuitous rings
about your being— I, balanced, entangled in love's swings.

Idleness

> *It is here, in idleness, I am real.*
> — Tu Fu

Being nothing goes with doing nothing,
the immaterial "I" forever incapable,
universally unable, my consciousness so close
to oblivion that absence of action seems
a satiation and satisfaction of human desire.

Motivated by age and illness to stay still,
I watch and wait awake and aware, excited
to be. Delighted to exist on the edge of death's
solemnity, alert to fires going out that youth
ignited, letting love of this world go unrequited.

In inebriating indolence, the aging process stops
and I am finally drunk on the wine of myself,
the fermenting hours of my stilled activity
producing vintage me: reclusive, exclusive,
pondering metaphysical profundities ego-free.

From the advantage plants have in staying put
to observe the universe from the vantage of
never roaming, ever in the same place, forever
viewing all things from one eternal perspective,
I can measure reality over which humans race.

It is here, in infinity, I am home. It is sincere,
this absence, this unmoving place, this abyss,
this halt in civilization's frenetic, human pace,
and I find the inert, the inactive mind empties
space/times' detritus, fills with reflective bliss.

I'm Tidying Up Things
With My Grandmother Again

I can see my breath so I know it's cold; only the
activity of going from garden to compost heap,
lugging decay from here to there, can keep
me warm these autumnal days— the old sun
wearily wheeling south, skimming a horizon
already in shadows bleached by distant haze.

I am in early evening now. And later, night.
Not much time remaining to heft a garden up
into sleep, separating what can come back
from so much lifeless dross gone to blight.
I do what I can, what's expected to be done,
reviewing summer, choosing what to prune,

what to bury in hopes of some resurrection
that will see green tendrils coil around June,
what to tear out with a summer of wisdom
backing me up, life I do not want to see again,
life too briefly pretty gone to weed too soon,
what to haul off permanently out of my ken.

She doesn't look over to me as she works
among the newly dead hollyhock stocks,
grabbing them sturdily by their long throats
and pulling hard, grabbing with both fists
those shocks of wheat-like weeds, wild oats,
puts her body bulkily against whatever resists.

I pause to watch her, wonder where she could
pull, tear next. I see her work her rhythms
along abelia, listen to her shears methodically
snip, clip summer-grown branchlets of wood
back to domestication, observe her clearly intent
on uncluttering sere autumn's falling curve.

Am I being ignored? She seems unaware
that she's not alone way out here in late fall,
not all alone in her determined way to serve
as a bringer of order to the end of a chaos
that began what seems like years ago in spring,
a chaos, a riot of music living seasons sing.

I call, but she doesn't hear. I would tell how
all this came to be: the flowers, the shrubs,
the vegetative nourishing of my human soul,
how I planted as the surest sign of civilization
as far as the eye can see. I started planting
years ago where thought and life align, go free.

As I have for well over half a century, I clean
the garden beds, clear the weeds, transplant
and stake new trees, working as I always have
beside her, feel her presence near and keen,
turn as she would turn to add to this pile or that,
putting this thatch to mulch, that batch to burn.

I know why she sees me not. I see her smile,
bend down, touch the boy I see now at her feet.
He's beautiful, and he smiles back as she twists
a root free, shows him how. He knows I'm here.
I see him look ahead to where I'll be standing,
musing, remembering in air come autumn-clear.

Angst Astride a Dragon

> *Rising and sinking for all time, an infinite process.*
> *Ignorant and wise alike succumb, finite their years.*
>   — Lu You

Innumerable darknesses of immemorial night
well up and surge, splash and splatter black, mark
illimitable territory of blank before birth, after death,
and we ourselves go deaf as we hark to our own cries,
lies we tell out of breath, lies that lash and scatter
as they leave our lips, lies steeped in awful religion
and culture that become whips with which we flagellate
body parts better kept hidden, dreams that form unbidden,
our private terrors and errors kicked up by this dragon
we are riding as they become dirt on us, become dust
blocking our view of the way as we hang on afraid,
beyond help or hurt toward extinction and release.

We cannot get off. We do not remember mounting.
It's just suddenly we were here, suddenly the dragon,
suddenly change, suddenly the lovely oblivion in which
we slept, suddenly the blank blanketing us was removed
and we were. We are. We ride on its back half mad
during erotic bursts and half sane with neurotic thirsts
after fleshy fulfillments only and ever sated and slaked
by changes bucking boredom of the stultifying status quo.
A dragon of change rears and rises with us on its back.
Our fright, our anxieties, our horrific attachments to life
are brief in the scheme of things in the eternal flow, and
a dragon brings luck to those awake enough to know.

See it slither and curl, twist and writhe, rear and roar;
dust flying off crumbling infrastructure of beliefs
as our world heaves, our histories are lost or rewritten
in new languages, our lives' denouements are tossed,
our petty plots and plans succumb to unforeseen griefs,
our fears overcome our pride as the dragon turns,
snarls, glares at us, and we, with nowhere to hide,
cling to its chaos as all we had hoped drowns, burns,
and we are left with an undeserved gift: opportunity.
We will put down fear. We will stand up and call
for a new day, see our way clear into a new paradigm
where we master our five senses and enjoy it all.

Adagio for Timpani

> *And thou, all-shaking thunder,*
> *Strike flat the thick rotundity of the world!*
> — William Shakespeare, King Lear

Who hasn't, long ago, heard sonorous, stentorian thunder roll
over oceans of air before oncoming storms looming black
across a far horizon, coming on in low baritone thunderation
and grumbling? Who hasn't lain supine in a summer field
while sunlight with its promises makes present pleasantness
seem mighty, when wildflowers all about begin to nod and bees
busy in ubiquitous clover cover themselves in freshening wind
rising, heralding an approaching, darkening, rumbling storm?

Does thunder's ominous omnipresence offer only acoustics,
nothing more, echoing off mountains' undulations, no one's affair?
Do white birds sky-high and soaring make but bright marks against
black storm banks coming on in their own slow time? Does wind
and rain birthed from the clouds' womb finally reach everyone
in adolescence addling self-reliance with an electric flash followed
by a finally arriving storm's reverberating orchestral crash and boom?
Does thunder move thought from self-satisfaction to surviving?

Who hasn't heard, coming upright out of a torpid, turgid sleep,
heaven's drum at two in the morning, the peal of hell shaking
we dead-to-the-world awake, white light having blinded night
a moment before? Who hasn't grasped the sullen percussion
of the skies rumbling after a lightning strike with power to shake
complacency for a moment and introduce a reverberating fright
that ends all discussion in lieu of a panic attack, for we believe
the hour is nigh when mayhem is certain and hope fades to black?

In night, in bed, in a young, callow lovers' arms, who has not felt
the heart's propensity to mimic timpani? The heart's dependency
on bliss? In night, naked night, lust-concealing, love-congealing
night, who hasn't heard pounding mounting in a lover's chest?
My god, is it all only fiery vibrations of deathless music echoing
the sounding heart, a clang of endorphin-inspired lyrics in the dark
down eons from calculating lust's own originating Big Bang—
this visceral thunder, sent by a god, storm-damaging and stark?

Before Dust Settled

An old photograph brushes dust from memory
and I am back to where we were when we were
briefly our own. Briefly dust-free. Innocently
ourselves and unbothered. Just seeds unsown.

Two-dimensional picture goes three-dimensional
in my mind, and we are together once more
laughing because we don't know any better,
touching because we are learning to adore.

We watch each other watch each other loving
life. Our new bodies. Earth. Space/time.
Laughter unforced. So little distance from birth,
was it only yesterday we rode oblivion's sublime?

I close my eyes. We are as we were again,
wind's song now as wind's song was then,
and bird calls I hear now are bird calls heard
in far fields long gone fallow way back when.

The photograph I touch now was touched
decades ago when it was new, just pulled fresh
from the camera, and it has yellowed but not
diminished, nor is it shorn of magic mellowed.

Gone, all that was flesh-born, innocent, finished,
and I realize here, here, with youth blown away,
with space/time buried under my decades of dust,
that dawn once sown cannot stay, cannot stay, with
age an additional line emptying all that age must.

Memory of a Shadow of a Fog

*The mind is not big enough
to hold a fortune.*
   — James Cihlar

Before life, like afterlife, beggars belief.
Where was I? And now how could I tell?
Before creation is blanker than after destruction.
Heaven, hell? Judgment, punishment, reward?
These are concepts of the mind, more simplistic
than all the world's sinful religions combined.

I only know this moment's miracle, territories
of history, blind guesses (none of them educated),
assumptions for tomorrow. But ask me about
existence before the womb, and I'll confess
I know as much about it as I do the tomb. Joy?
Sorrow? What of them before birth or after death?
Was there or will there be such a thing as a toy,
a tool, an importance leading to abated breath?

I see clouds. I see mist twirling, vaporous, gauzy,
insubstantial, and evanescing; furling, unfurling,
a watery sky as dew-point dependent for existence
as a zygote-to-be is dependent on a lover's sigh.

I know spun-sugar-like, cotton-candy-like,
unspooling arabesques of moisture spiraling, curling,
curlicues of ethereality. I see them coming down,
silent, restive. See them seep through atmosphere,
hover over open oceans, yet repose around, above,
and through a city, a town, a forest, a field. See them
swirl, abound. See them seem unreal in streetlight,
churning in a quietude, rolling, swaying grey plumes
and splaying about all things, touching them yet
not touching them, nowhere or afar a moment ago
but now here briefly masking sun, moon, and stars,
then nowhere again except what little's left in tricky
memory. The thought "Always" surrounds infinity,
but I see that though I am, I was not, nor will I be.

What Will He Get?

> *He wants this moment in the body,*
> *to feel there the pleasure it holds,*
> *and then whatever it is that pleasure*
> *leaves behind . . .*
>   — David Watts

He wants a lot . . . and all of it fleeting, fleeing time
that races after flesh as flesh itself races after passion.

He wants his body to bask as if in Eden, to know the sublime,
to love as if in Sodom in some despotic, erotic fashion.

He wants to be immersed in lust and orgasm's climatic song
sung loudly and defiantly in the face of man-made gods.

He wants to be proudly sybaritic, however it may be wrong,
his youth surviving experience's repetitions, whatever the odds.

He wants what's left after lust, love, life; what may be called
the dregs of space and time, the ashes of passion fulfilled.

He wants erotica forever, given half a chance; time stalled
in joy of an act ever mythic that magic gods have willed.

He wants, then, to submerge in his memory's sacred dust,
feel the emptiness of aging recollection when time shall pass.

He wants to know what pleasure leaves behind: the dirt, the rust,
the sadness and hurt of his five senses heading beneath the grass.

Gold Dust

> *Last night, the east wind again blew through*
> *my small dwelling, bringing unbearable nostalgia . . .*
>   — Li Yu

I turn to find your cardigan folded as you left it
across the back of your recliner, as if awaiting
the hour of your return. It will wait a long time.

I learn from your wallet on our dresser how to wait
quietly. Your wristwatch, tickless, silently explains
grief does not abate, nor is relief in what remains.

Emptiness is everywhere attached to everything
that was yours, including me. Even the surf
sounding off our harbor rocks echoes hollowly.

Your chair is as vacant as my grief-stricken stare,
and I would fill it again with you, again and again
seeing you there nonchalant, taking up life anew.

Your side of our bed hurts with the impossibility
of ever being refilled. I can't lie in it, as it awaits
an emptying of my side to join it infinitely stilled.

Your clothes rest in peace, closeted, put away,
their being out of sight allowing me to pretend
a momentary normalcy as grief and life descend.

And descend they do, grief of love, grief of life,
into evening cold, dust of this world weakening,
deepening, though some of this dust be gold.

Hey, Billy

What is it, to remember nothing, of what one loved?
To have forgotten the faces one first kissed?
 — Chen Chen

Hey, Billy, did you ever think we'd be this old?
Was it a curse or just another human happenstance
that let years run askew and awry, amok and away
from those nights we made love in our unholy dark,
from those days clotted with ignorance and romance,
from our hands all over each other in arousing play,
and into adulthood's painful theatrics false and stark,
and into memory beyond reach of aging and dismay?

Hey, Billy, let the decades sleep. Love is unforgotten.
Hey, Billy, let the dust settle and all of space/time creep
toward its inevitable oblivion, without the preservation
of a single kiss that once fired promises too hot to keep,
for you and I remember everything of erotic wrestlings
without reservation: metaphysical, paradisiacal and deep.

Adagio for a Young Cousin

for David

Decades (too many) separate us from being buddies,
but in Elizabethan times, that's what cousins were:
friends close enough to be family, comrades bonded
tight enough to care, pals who've got each other's back
and who'd shed blood willingly in an honorable affair.

In my 70s, I'm sailing on a different tack from yours,
my course bearing me away over oceans of imagination
toward harbors on The Other Side that religions mapped
inaccurately but seductively, space/time here shortened
as I shorten sails and apply my wisdom to all that's apt.

In your youth, you're sailing on a different tack from mine,
your course bearing you along coasts of life's tropic paradise
with wide bays, beaches of sharp sand both white and fine,
palm-shaded inlets waiting to be explored nakedly, wantonly,
as unwise youth should explore in the prime of salad days.

Wisdom would unmake you. There will be time for that.
For now, you must savor sensually in erotic celebrations,
unworried by your reckless heart racing over tides of life
footloose, feckless, callow, ripping innocence from your
flesh and cutting away customs with your intellect's knife.

Even from this growing distance as I disappear in pieces,
it's fun to watch you, an Alexander conquering the world
as if no one had been here before you, raising a banner
to claim new experiences imperially for young humanity,
as if such an egoistic banner had never before been unfurled.

Your music is loud, rapid, heavy metal, written for horns, while mine is soft, slow, new age, and written for strings (heavy on cellos). I suppose we could briefly compromise on a saxophone, but for me it would have to be tenor and playing a sensuous air of fleshy solace, intimate goodbyes.

There's no plain-speaking, age to youth. But your beauty is a canticle to the power of The Big Bang, and I cannot pass by on my way hither, thither, and yon without touching your shoulder, and when you've grown older, you'll recall a serious song sung once in loving admiration, then gone.

Old in a Dust Storm

The rose dies, man dies, the world dies, the god
grows and fails, the born universe dies
   into renewal,
and all endures the change,
totally lost and totally retained.
   — A. R. Ammons

Even what I've finished remains incomplete,
what I would've said unsaid, would've done undone,
my sleep replete with dreams undreamt,
my waking, aching hours spent worrying,
my tidy philosophies of life in fact unkempt.

My mind would shed my corrupted flesh,
rid itself of pain and wrangling anguish,
to view the world afresh as when the body
was young and dominated the day, its future
existed, and once found, love would stay.

My consciousness would shed my mind,
let everything five senses brought for thought
disappear down the universe's rabbit hole
along with space/time, leaving oblivion for me,
absence, emptiness, Eden: I, existence-free.

Sequel

Yet Ah, that Spring should vanish with the Rose!
That Youth's sweet-scented manuscript should close!
        — Edward FitzGerald

The script that youth writes is bold, smooth, sharply lined
with ink as dark as blood is hot, with letters that slant
along straight rows that seem as if they'd run time out of mind
through the blood and bone of fresh experience, but flesh can't
last the length of language, histories that run and never end,
tales of lust and loves and laughter only youth can tell,
as youth is prone to odysseys and fancies, as youth will wend
through space/time as if it were a place only youth can dwell.

Another manuscript of life follows youth's sweet-scented book:
age's chronicles and canticles come after youth's lyric pages,
written in elderly scrawl and blotted, stained with lines askew,
written to instruct light-hearted youth in experience's wages
ignored by the young as they pursue things hurriedly and blind,
the aged epistles showing how each body finally lies resigned.

Spring Dreams in Autumn

*A sudden spring dream
crowded with my years,
the past so far, so far.*
— Ou-yang-Hsiu

In being's last chapter, I look back:
where I've been, what I've become,
distancing me from passions of yore,
my current, unenviable self numb
with only a serenity of ashes in store.

In dreams I am young again, although
with wisdom I did not possess back then,
and my present experience is incongruous
with my once-buff innocence, my dreams
twisted without reference to where or when.

I stuff my long-past spring dreams with
dubious acts of my later summer years,
but I remember, I remember, and though
my dreams decay as my dissolution nears,
I take pride in my loves, abide my tears.

What troubles these spring dreams of mine
is my long-lost contact with what I was,
for summer sundered innocence necessary
to believe, to hope, to imagine myself worthy
to receive license to repeat splendors in old age.

I know too much. I've become too wise
to deceive myself with five senses' fairytales
and I grieve in my unsanitary dreams for lies
that made me happy, kept me callow, and
youthful traces remain around my goodbyes.

So, far, so far! I've only spring dreams
occurring in my life's late autumn sleep
to recall my early yearnings for satisfactions
I now know are reserved for oblivion only,
notwithstanding crowded years' lonely sweep.

Dragonfly

> *I couldn't decide how I felt about the world*
> *but the blue and green lush of it somehow keeps me going*
>   — Laurie MacFayden

Ill and old, ill and old, I see daffodils yellow still,
their flared trumpets blaring young spring's silence
in my ears overwhelmed by human fuss and noise.

My cancerous chaos and cardiac confusion day to day
do not hinder my flow and float in space/time's joys,
and in my mind's eye I see me as I was along the way.

In a slackening current, I may be approaching the sea,
my consciousness regaining its place amid its waves,
and as riverbanks fall away, I am to a lesser degree

susceptible to civilization's rants and raves, perceiving
a botanical world's offerings of love, an animal world's
rotations, raptures, the world of Homo sapiens deceiving.

In spite of asphalt, meadows come back tan and green.
In spite of concrete, beaches return to stone and sand.
In spite of steel, plains revert to beauty previously unseen.

As if made by Lalique, there glides above an ink-like pool
a work of fatal, natal art that rides on reality's still air
wreaking sudden eternity on some, this quick-killing jewel.

As if made by Cartier, there lifts above a darkening field
a needle massive in its implications for the life of flies,
a rupture of cosmic rapture to which such things yield.

As if made by Tiffany, there rises above human destitution,
on amethyst-emerald wings, change signaled by a dragon-
fly cutting havoc among gnats that sing, that sting, that die.

Ars Moriendi

> *My hair all white, goosefoot cane: what joy,*
> *mind and life gone perfectly transparent!*
>   — Tu Fu

And what an art it is, this dying, this slow turning away
from physicality and its obsessions with space/time,
from the musicality of the heart in love, concerns of clay,
weevils of hours eating the beautiful fabric of youth,
leaving songs of this world for silence of what comes next,
relieving evils of religion masking oblivion's truth,
receiving common sense at last from blood's ancient text
that says dying is consciousness's ending of all pretense.

There, in dying's art, we find revelation and transparency,
immortality of the metaphysical, clarity our recompense
for the material world's confusion and consciousness's parity
with the chaotic flux and flow of ultimate absence existing
before us, after us, within us, inside and outside space/time,
the art of dying being the cornerstone of change's shrine.

Adagio for the Oort Cloud

Jan Oort knew something of how quickly from nothing
an amazement appears rolling, tumbling, coming forth
straight at you, and you are going to be changed forever
once it arrives— a phenomenon inconceivable until then,
a circumstance a stolid, staid status quo never survives.

Surrounded as you are in a black, blank spherical void,
you only see what far light from stars reveals: birthing
galaxies, swirling galaxies, galaxies destroyed, all from
forces of quantum size when a quantum world congeals
and hardens and orbits unseen, unknown, unformed.

Look up at the night sky. Look up in daylight. You see
not a trace, not a hint of their anonymous billions, their
autonomous powers of concentration, their concentrically
whirling, waiting, resting willy-nilly in your outer fears,
abiding beyond rationalization in your humdrum hours.

Hard to imagine, by their billions they float unwarmed,
tiny humanity unaware of even their nebulosity. Almost
outside of understanding, asteroids reside like thoughts
from calm to dire, from innocence to harm, ice to fire,
from circling there untapped, undiscovered, dark, bare.

Like a thought it comes streaking from out of nowhere,
from a place of which you were ignorant, and sudden
knowledge stuns— a thought that had never occurred
to you arriving, shot headlong into your cerebral cortex,
your adored world not surviving its absurd enormity.

One minute you're complacent, self-satisfied, even bored,
the next you're turned to stone by an idea both radical
and demanding that roared through your psyche, and now
you're seeing cultural norms and political correctness
struck blind as you stagger under a concept seconds ago

the furthest thing from your mind, seconds ago blasphemy,
seconds ago impossible to be your future on Planet Earth.
You, awestruck with the rest of your superficial kind,
will rise in dust of the realization that's fallen upon you,
never again as intellectually inert under such active skies.

Dusting

My grandmother taught me how to dust
so long ago it's hard to remember now,
but it's memory I trust, memory I know,
memory that seasons my life at this remove,
and memory that provides me reasons.

First, she said, look. See what is and isn't
dusty and plan your time. Walk in nature,
rivers and mountains with removes of sky,
and wend away from human gatherings
to feel what is to be born, what is to die.

Then, she said, look. See where dust falls
and if you can bear it, for dust is everywhere
collecting on creation's furniture and frailties.
Flow into yourself, and there, go detecting,
inspecting what's worth your time and care.

Dust is on a surface only, hides a sheen,
collects on top of the otherwise sublime,
deepens if not removed, cheapens all
evaluations of what might lie beneath
until objects disappear under its pall.

Down it falls, 24/7, 52 weeks of the year,
day and night descending like hours themselves
falling softly on times of gold, times of lead,
covering sanity and insanity, silencing thought,
erasing hierarchies of the quick and the dead.

Let it. Let it be so. Take yourself away
and into the clarity of hindsight and dreams
by dusting metaphysical surfaces of your mind,
trusting your consciousness to see what seems
isn't what is, knowing five senses most unkind.

In mental swirls and pirouettes, twirls and regrets,
wipe clean experience, belief, space/time's flow,
keeping above culture's cognitions and grime,
sleeping through humanity's quotidian traffic,
leaping inward toward love powering the sublime.

Incarnations

I'd like to get away from earth awhile
And then come back to it and begin over.
   — Robert Frost

Ruffling through memory, shuffling dust of experience,
I recall little I knew as an adolescent, less as a child.
Huffing and puffing through adulthood, I soiled
my intellect with dogma and dicta filmy and flimsy,
foiled the goal my consciousness may have had when
abruptly I fell into space/time, my five senses' whimsy
taking precedence over the high purposes of my mind.

Covered over with civilization's unfathomable dust,
embowered in rooms filled with cultured detritus,
deflowered by experience's dirt, in dirt, for dirt,
my essence discovered alert only when accompanied
by lust, by the many, many erotica of imagination;
I am ready for departure, for a letting go, for a while
to pause consciousness and lie inconspicuous in flow.

Knowing what I know, or rather surmising what I surmise,
not proving as a scientist but believing as a metaphysician,
let me come back newly clean as new seed in a new spring;
let me be wise as only the hollow, the empty are wise;
let me reconnoiter and reconquer space/time once more
sealing myself into flesh and flexibility as I did of yore,
but this time doing it up right, feeling what I didn't before.

Let me come back, begin over in ignorance, innocence,
my mind's eye blind, my flesh unscorched by desires,
my character no longer treating other consciousnesses
as if I were a priority, a singularity the universe admires.
Let me come back, begin over, running amok and amain
through space/time unlearned, my imagination aflame,
egoless, spurning acclaim— I, returning chastened, sane.

Youth's Departure

A mad wind drives rain across March night.
I close the door against the dusk,
but find no way to hold the spring.
— Ou-yang Hsiu

It will leave, spring, the way youth leaves:
turning, returning, seeming not to leave at all,
pausing on the sill of departure to blow a kiss
remembered later in nostalgia's imperfect thrall
as a farewell token as it exited the year, a life,
letting us ponder aging's ways of breaking bliss.

A mad passion drives pain across aging's plight.
We will grow old. We will grow old. Spring
abandons us who once were callow and blind
to where those bold roads youth trod would lead,
evolving cold roads that become stark, unkind,
lark-light roads darkening as spring's joys recede.

We try to close a door against inevitable night,
but flesh's candles once tall and strong and bright
now gutter, their flames aflicker and smoking
as they burn down and out, and those of us wise
re-open that door to let candled flesh blow out
as we hope in the dark, raise our arms to the skies.

Congenital Myopia

In my sodden, quiet, quite terminal December,
mind indoors and out of body's winter weather,
mind trying to stay warm while body, well,
body grasps, clings, and wraps itself as best it can —
in my gray, stolid, solid December way, I see
my April self dreaming of the day he'd be a man.

He wants toy soldiers to be real things, his toy cars
drivable, his plastic weapons to be gleaming steel,
his warm nights suitable for more than watching stars;
his April is more than ready to molt into May
where he hopes his fears of doing nothing, being
nothing, will dissipate grandly in his coming years.

Some nights, in bed alone, nude alone, he pretends
his pillow loves him and proposes secret sins
that he's certain no one has thought of before,
and some nights an undertone of adult fires
warms him blood and bone, and he yearns for
close companions who approve his new desires.

Now and then, anguished by his youth, he peers
into his future; stressed by shedding adolescence,
he jeers at restrictions imposed and policed;
pressed by hormones and endorphins, he fears
time is not on his side and his life will be closed,
have passed by before he's had his chance to fly.

He chafes at childhood's last, soft manacles
that, before he knows it, will fall away to leave
him free to be whoever, wherever, whatever
he's pleased to be. He looks into his future
seeing vastness, greatness, Eros, Zeus, Apollo,
although, I can assure you, he isn't seeing me.

Those Who Knew Me
When My World Was Young

Sometimes in late evening, or early morning,
when the moon is right, I talk to them.
Sometimes in early evening, or late morning,
when the mood is right, I walk with them.

They know how I was, what I am now,
what my journey was, and when and how
things came together or fell apart to create
the song I am that space/time briefly sings.

My teachers made an effort, did their best,
and cannot be blamed for where I didn't
meet their standards or failed their test,
my consciousness ever to remain untamed.

My young friends must be finally amazed
to see me totter, hear me sigh and declaim
my old age's gravity as I wander dazed by all
that happened to me– I, never to be the same.

The burly trees of my early days are gone
to rot, lumber, or what suffices for tree heaven,
but they ghost around me now, leafing shade for
my mind where human dogma and dicta slumber on.

My childhood's gone dogs have never left me,
paw the passages of my wan memory's heart,
and they nuzzle me as encouragement to kindness
even where mindlessness forces people apart.

When they were young, they and I, the world
wobbled less and human laws rang true as we
played rowdily raucous under a hawkless sky
where all was safe and space/time was new.

They are here with me despite disappearances
of us all, and they answer my concerns about
the future (mine and theirs) with a lovely silence
speaking volumes in the perpetuity that age learns.

Winter Dragon

And so with the winter solstice the lake freezes over
and with a coat of snow, everyone who wasn't here
in warmer weather would think it's a field of clover
gone to rest under drifts until warmer days reappear.

But the Chinese dragon knows. And the dragon lies
curled about itself at the bottom of the cold lake,
its passion furled with all its somnolence implies
until some undisclosed time ahead for life's remake.

Not senescent, not deliquescent, the dragon rests
oblivious to those ice fishermen and skaters above
unknowingly touching a world where a dragon nests
to wait out winter doldrums before spring's shove.

Only change is eternal, its motion creation, a flow
that writhes and turns as it wends and churns away
snake-like, with consciousness coming to know
change is an impartial but thorough molder of clay.

But hold! A dragon is not dormant nor does it sleep.
Even under water in winter it sees. Even in this cold,
it treats reality with metaphysics, knowing life will keep
burgeoning, and dragons, like change, never grow old.

Lying on a pond's bottom, a lake's deep, dark side,
the winter dragon ruminates on where and how and why
spring will come and urges rise for a dragon to glide
to the surface of everything, more change coming nigh.

Oh you, straying from custom, playing for a moment
by a placid pond, quiet lake, slow river, or soft sea,
know this: nothing is forever. Chinese dragons foment
change, even in winter never letting space/time be.

Oh you, about to be bowled over by chance events
unforeseen, inescapable diagnoses, accidents, and such;
oh you, who are unaware of cares no prayer prevents,
await a dragon's thrash and splash, clutch and touch.

A winter dragon cogitates as fierce winter snow flies
while humans begin to doubt the coming of spring,
but metaphysics is real and a frozen winter lake belies
spectacular interruptions a waiting dragon sets to bring.

Immortality

> *... the past and present I think are one ....*
> — Wei Ying-wu

I'm connected to my yesterday self, yesteryear self,
all the way back and into the womb, all of me
united seamlessly, my previous hours on a shelf
of memory but no less real, still in existence, riding
along with me as I talk, smell, taste, see, and feel.

Merely because myself in my past cannot change,
cannot rearrange, cannot do anything not done then,
does not mean my past self isn't there, isn't alive
in time's fourth dimension with a wisdom of Zen,
myself in my past fully engaged and fully aware.

Death only terminates my line of selves moving
through time, truncating my flesh's future affair
but not erasing the existence of people no longer
incandescent in the present, but still eternally there
and being and knowing and enjoying with a will.

Myself in the past kisses loves and lovers as before,
always a first time, always new, always and forever
as fresh as the moment that has long past into yore,
and myself in the past raises his arms to the sky
in praise of what was and is and will be when I die.

Being in a Garden

> *Conquer the world by not meddling.*
> — Lao Tzu

Real, suddenly, they are: these sunlit plants,
these dew-moist plants in their silent, silent green.
Feel the moment, for space/time in its enormity
grants few such small slices of stasis between
coming and going, inhale and exhale of breath,
arriving and departing, human birth and death.
Sigh, if you must, with a tinge of regret that you
cannot stay for long in Eden, but celebrate
that you're here now, that your five senses
allow you to know joy in how quantum physics
produces the Table of the Elements and you.

Even weeds implore your notice, insisting
ugliness is a matter of perspective, wanting you
to ignore your upbringing of bias, intolerance,
hate wielded against a green and silent minority
that can only pray to escape notice, shielded
by lying low, the underground a safer place
to spread ambitious roots, or by where they grow,
raising shoots of life away from crops and lawns,
or by producing a trillion seeds that survive terrain
as forsaken as the flanks of Mars's Olympus Mons,
until they can reproduce and repopulate their ranks.

Douglas-fir, hemlock, and western mountain pine
are a massed palisade walling in this earthy Eden
minus snakes, although the Tree of Knowledge
of the Difference Between Good and Evil thrives.

Inhale, exhale fresh air of a cool morning, keen
to feel joy in your regular breathing, heartbeat,
pulse rate, and five senses all telling you the truth
for once. Sigh and repeat. Smile and repeat.
High branches of green needles in hefty swags
droop and rise above and around you; sparrows
call, loop, flit, and drift in Whitman's lacy jags.

Rhododendrons rule, banks of their humongous
blossoms flanking walkways leading to wisteria,
their pendulous blue florescence in flower just
for you at this time and place, your stress receding
as you pause, finally, to accept, marvel, and trust
for once in your life that vegetation is life, too,
is friendship, is kinship in being and needing
on the same level, at the same intensity, as you;
and see where the path has led you to water lilies
and lotus, koi twisting, sliding against them and
each other in profusions of accepting, insisting.

Put fingers to the scalloped leaves of ocean spray
and know a thing can be both soft and rough,
delicate and tough, hold fast in horrific wind
and yet sway gently in a slight breeze enough
to cause its white cascades to splash and foam
against its branches as if against a rocky shore,
as if happiness were merely being at home
in a garden of menial delights, mental delights;
sprigs of ocean spray telling you in their way
to make up your mind to be soft and rough,
delicate and tough, hold fast, seize your day.

How silent are the foxgloves, cathedral spires
of lavender, purple and white towering above
swirls of thick emerald leaves, and their desires

are simple and pure: to spill a billion tiny seeds
unseen into the garden duff, their slim beauty
belying their toxins as they stand by your walk,
and the foxgloves are not demure, do not hide,
will not pretend, and they conquer survival
by being a quiet poison wherever they abide,
and they call to you as you pass: "Stay pure.
Don't fight the world. Be clay. Play. Endure."

See where field bindweed climbs ceanothus,
bindweed pretending to be morning glory,
its white bugles blaring superiority, triumph,
its thin tendrils encoiling the California lilac's
fading blue blooms, the garden the better for it,
two very different messengers sent to say
in very different body language how good it is
to cling, to be clung to, to be together should
winds blow, rains wash away, suns burn,
and they are always there for you, always
aware of this blessing when fortunes turn.

Wind in the elderberry causes their jade leaves
to wave, "Come on!" Tossing spindles of
Indian plum in early bloom hail your passing.
Your consciousness receives benedictions
from liriope and sweet woodruff massing
at your feet. Variegated vinca vines thread
through sky blue chicory spread beneath
arcs and arches of bridalwreath spirea wed
to spring, larks in song opening awareness
to operatic summer's entrance before long,
larks choiring a cathedral space/time strong.

Columbine raises blue, silent bells along
a meandering path whose end ahead lies

hidden as it turns lightly, darkly, here and there,
hither, thither and yon, like your own way
out of this present moment, this hour, this day
in which you lie perfectly afloat and aware,
garden path and your path intersecting once,
here, and you should take notice, ignoring
glare and glitter of civilization's insignificance
compared to this garden's opening onto
Oblivion in which all things lie ensnared.

Japanese red pine, Japanese black pine,
their rust, their coal contortions streaking
inky lines across a temporarily blue sky;
Japanese red pine, Japanese black pine,
their forked thrust up from a garden's base
reaches for the metaphysical in you,
touches your consciousness. Trust their
needle-tassels to disturb the human universe
that clutches your attention, your energy,
to provoke a mild if sudden understanding
that peace, acceptance, life, love are wild.

Even with no moon in a night of absence,
even in the dark, no star guiding, no breath
of air stirring invisible flowers in the ever
indivisible blackness, blankness there,
still floral fragrances rise to you to answer
your sighs, your heart's innermost cries,
for your questing consciousness still seeing
plies the metaphysical range of your being,
relies on life in all its forms to hear the song
silently sung to you forever: "You belong."

Let autumn come. Let winter rule. Let chill
dominate the garden gone gray and ashen,

foliage now duff, flowers lost to memory,
when even the happiest heart has had enough
of ice and snow and wondering where things
young and bright and sensual have gone,
for consciousness will know life among
space/time's finite pleasures is not long,
their songs quickly sung, their treasures fail,
and yet the garden is still there in nothingness
ready to be again when creative forces prevail.

Every tree, shrub, flower, and lowly plant
is telling you they know. They share. They, too,
float and drift and become aware. They, too,
appreciate and applaud. And they care for you.
It was your own god you made in your image
and not the Garden of Eden that bade you go.
"Hallelujah," the garden says to you in silence.
"Hosannah," the garden says to you in innocence.
"Our bodies, like your body, are destined
for absence, but we ourselves are not. Like you,
we are perennials in metaphysical thought."

Nothing says it right like the Plant Kingdom,
ever essential, ever a base for all else's
flourishing, nourishing every other phenom
from the Table of the Elements that alights
on the surfaces of a reality only stars can hone.
Bright, calm, stalwart in their stationary stance,
silently supportive of your being there alone
in their crowd-free delights, proud of romance,
gardens give to your presence their tint and tone,
melding with consciousness to be space/time's
ultimate essence: wisdom in blood and bone.

Purgatory

> *Quite a task,*
> *putting together Heaven, yet we do.*
> —James Merrill

You see an old man as he is: frail, flaccid, failing
to thrive, thinning hair, dimming eyes, querulous,
pale, standing with a vacant stare in a beggar's guise
as physically unattractive as a beast in a fairytale,
and you see his physicality, Eros diminished, chaste,
a fool, no one in his right mind interested in this aged
waste, a man of no use as a tool for any purpose,
an obtuse mortal in whom decay and dissolution rule.

I'll not dread what life allots and five senses allow.
I've earned wisdom I've put to use as youth has fled,
and learned Eden's architecture and drafted heaven
in my mind, even now imagination-crafted dreams
lifting me up, ready to sip from the cup of oblivion
to taste reality and know really that death redeems.

Intellect as Companion

> *... tonight*
> *my life is an old friend sitting with me ...*
> — Richard Blanco

Here with you in your aging's private wilderness
which we eke through one angst after the other,
we yet dream big. Keep me in your confidence as if
I were the only true friend you've ever had. Hug me
as if I've ever been the only true love toward which
your heart beckoned. I didn't stop it from breaking,
for I didn't know how. But surely your pain in our
joined ebb and flow was vital to getting us here now,

ever the two of us, shoulder to shoulder, going it alone
to where imagination teases the two of us intertwined,
the two of us pulled together by rough experience,
we being joined at the hip metaphysically, a fact
defying science or an easy existence, you needing me
to do everything you'd do, me needing you to act.

Don't you remember when I joined you in the womb?
How happy you were, how surprised, and we feasted
from your mother's blood, breathed your mother's air,
took stock, then slipped hand-in-hand into sunlight.
Slapped hard into this world, we first cried together,
and the umbilical cord cut didn't sever you from me,
for we romped, raged, relished, recanted through years
well-met, filled, and stored, and now we let them be.

Next? Time slackens, gets fuzzy edges, appalls,
and we see omens, loomings, separation in the offing
after much between us, you going a mortal's way.
Here in your gray waiting, crying your parting calls,
remember the physical world we kept as comrades
sharing the mortal blessing, now sharing its decay.

Last Illusions

Dream delivers us to dream,
and there is no end to illusion.
   — Ralph Waldo Emerson

And so I have come to here and now,
stumbling in the dark of a lamp gone out
that once may have been lifted briefly
beside a golden door, muttering to myself,
upbraiding myself, punishing myself
for not listening, not having done more
on so many levels on so many issues; ego,
like flesh, having pulchritude, glistening.

I can close my eyes anytime I want and
I'm there: the child, the seeker, the sleeper
who wasted the dark, again a boy unaware.
I was ignorant, which is to say, innocent.
Once again, I'm the brother whose keeper
no one is, again the stranger not taken in.

Hymn to Yesterday's Gods

Great God! I'd rather be
a pagan suckled in a creed outworn . . .
have sight of Proteus rising from the sea;
or hear old Triton blow his wreathed horn.
      — Wordsworth

Thank you. You filled the bill until we came
to our senses and used our senses to explore
and understand space/time, to establish order
on our own, to explain all before science gave us
the real universe defined, with Eden, Nirvana,
Utopia, and Elysian Fields existing in the mind.

Like fine art, the creation can be no better or worse
than its creator, whether picture, music, or verse;
whether naiad, dryad, angel or devil, goddess or god,
so it's not your fault if we made you self-satisfied,
given to curse, given a lust for sadism to sate, fear
of other gods, and a penchant for egotism and hate.

Made in our image, you were as attractive as we
wanted ourselves to be— albeit somewhat aloof,
a bit paranoid, envious, and cruel, and we used you
as a crutch to get through each day, religion as a tool,
divinity as hope, belief in fairytales a proven way
to face unknowns, the unknowable infinite in scope.

We put words into your mouths, wrote your laws,
and looking at you was looking into a mirror
miraculous in reflection. We gave our applause
to what we saw, sang hosannahs and gave esteem,
worshiping not what you are but what you seem,
all of us willing to die for our self-created cause.

All slaying we committed in a god's name allowed
both praying and preying to be equal, free of blame,
and we fashioned holy dogma to color our justice
as we came to see our myth-like fiction as real,
as we came to ensure your friction with science
ended in your favor beyond evidence's appeal.

Theologies of hunter/gatherers, doxologies of tribes
took us out of the Stone Age into the Anthropocene,
and religion was our documentation that described
the world in which we finally came to believe,
never our intent to harm but rather our attempt
to charm, to guide, to strengthen our resolve
to do good, let love abide, and never to deceive.

We matured. We endured. We came to see
what we'd done in some god or other's name
was what profited those of us who ruled, and
to those of whom we made enemies went blame,
to those of whom we envied went shame, and
to those of us who were not fooled it was a game.

Reality, literally, is what we make it. Once,
in our youth, we romanced gods into being,
sought to control happenstance with songs
and danced before altars to gods all-seeing,
and we were carnal and we were venal, and we
loved good fortune that miracles brought to be.

Then decade by decade, century by century,
era by era, our holy stories aged, yellowed,
became antiquated and eventually silly
in the light of science as humanity mellowed,
became less tribal, less self-centered with less
reliance on magic of sacrament and bible.

And yet, and yet . . . beautiful Hermes, Shiva,
Saint John the Beloved, Balder, and Amun-Ra:
where has our hunt for immortal beauty gone?
Aphrodite, Virgin Mary, Parvati, and Freyja:
your loveliness we surely miss in our stress,
and thus in holy bliss your images linger on.

How simple was our faith, how soon understood
were the chance and chaos of this world;
our trust in you, our own creations, a boon
to our survival, a romance of our imagination,
our naivete groomed for fairytales, for a penchant
to worship objects, objets d'art, sun and moon.

Goodbye to Genesis, Ecclesiastes, and Revelations.
We sigh for simplicity in our bowers of space/time.
We cry for justice and mercy and right and wrong.
We would repeal science and release the far stars
to go back to our ignorance when flesh was strong.
Rest in our still-seeking hearts where gods belong.

It's Not Dementia

One can see what will trouble this sleep of mine,
whatever sleep it is.
Were he not gone, the woodchuck could say whether
it's like his long sleep, as I describe its coming on,
or just some human sleep.
    — Robert Frost

For the life of me, I can't get used to seeing old friends
gone for years visiting me at odd moments, their being
dead no barrier at all to their attentive listening to me,
then disappearing as if they were never here beside me,
their smiles as warm as ever, their bodies as healthy
as they were long ago when we were young humanity.

The walk may be asphalt to you, but to me, I walk on
a soft woodsy duff as I reach out, not for that steel pole,
but for a black birch that grew old beside my school,
that grows there still in my timeless, faultless mind,
and even now its bold, lenticellated bark feels cool
to my hand though you see metal from where you stand.

My birdfeeders, where are they? Where did I put seed?
Here in my room, I search for small things that stray
and are lost to you, but not to me, and I need their feel
between my fingers: rings, coins, photographs, and such
that trigger scenes that seem to be current still and I'm
in them as I was back then: young, robust with a will.

Strings of long-ago conversations yet come to mind.
I try to carry them on even though I know I'm alone
and who knows who's listening? Things I wished
I'd said, I say now, hoping those who aren't here

still can hear, those who mattered once can know
I haven't forgotten them though time has shattered.

The past is a better place than here, and I dust off
memories to be back bright again in my world of yore
where I was whole and strong, and still am in my
mind's eye where there are no stone strangers,
no corridors that lead nowhere I want to go, and I
live inside a blown reverie of what was until I die.

Auld Lang Syne

Now the New Year reviving old Desires,
The thoughtful Soul to Solitude retires . . . .
— Edward FitzGerald

A massive old year passes with banked fires
that once burned immoderately with emotion
and titillated the five senses from joy to dismay
and scintillated the heart's heaven with stars
that were hours of love-making and wild play
before old age jars pleasure's bowers with decay.

A massive bold year of raising dust and desire
is passing into yore, which is to say oblivion,
its days ice-cold, its nights ash, its waters a mire
that once was a lake fed by rivers of space/time
where all good things were fresh, flesh, and afire
with passion to pursue attainment of the sublime.

A massive told year is silent now, the story done,
its chronicles and canticles put away for sleeping,
its tales, once anticipated with glee, are spoken
and there's nothing more to say under the sun
that rose and set on bustling people busy keeping
appointments of no matter, for their races are run.

A massive extolled year is finished with praise,
its accomplishments furnished with nouns and verbs
for scholars of history to preach lessons that amaze
children of no experience with acts of no consequence,
space/time having moved on, leaving this year behind
in a candle's guttering, an old life's puttering mind.

New year? Whence does it come? How soon gone.
In a trice or less, in time it takes night to follow dawn,
it, too, will be old. First bold, then told, extolled
once it, too, passes, becoming quiet, faded, static,
its tinsel tarnished from misuse and misconception,
a new year at birth destined for jaded history's attic.

The thoughtful soul, the ruminating soul retires
from calendars long before death requires a farewell,
long before consciousness discards flesh's lore,
long before imagination tires and loves close;
the wiser soul hearing the eternally tolling bell
summoning each consciousness to infinite repose.

What If It Comes as a Sleeping?

> *What the mind creates, the body suffers.*
> — Yung-chia

Not as a gunshot? Not as a knife thrust
deep into vitals and then a twist, a pain
as horrific as cancer doing its level worst
to bust every organ open, stoicism slain,
all bits of religious dicta and dogma burst?

What if instead it arrives as a calming?
What if one eases into willing submission
finding nothing to dread, nothing alarming?
What if hospitalization were unnecessary,
and it were enjoyed sans chilling inhibition?

Not as a hobgoblin? Not as a terrorist awry
in the inner workings of one's brain; rather
as one's first love returning, returning,
promising love in silence, solace, by and by
your early lust's lyrics in a new fleshy refrain?

What if it reveals where it has always been?
What if it has been resting decades within?
A natural part of one? Quiet? Manifesting
what metaphysics should have taught one of
oblivion being alpha and omega of all questing?

Shall I close my arms as I close my eyes?
Shall I smile? If I be naked, what of it?
What if music plays in my mind all the while?
What if it comes as sunlit, moonlit dreaming,
this nothingness of death and ultimate denial?

... And They Lived Happily Ever After

And we did indeed, dying slowly as we all die
after our great moments in our space/time lives,
dying softly, deftly, almost minus notice, freely
partaking of silence and dark where calm thrives,
drinking nectar of first autumnal, then winter rain,
eating ambrosia of metaphysics, consciousness
inside dying bodies waking to their immortality;
we two consciousnesses holding aching hands,
leaning into each other for solace and sustenance
against space/time's immorality, while age expands
our view of what's to come, what's to be, ourselves
together in a great river's froth and foam, ourselves
together late into evening, ourselves our wine,
our feast, everything we remember newly vivid
as we find ourselves at this late hour to be song:
ethereally and quantumly entangled ever together
even after our lifetime's loving coupling's gone.

On Your Finding I'm Gone

for Ralph

Space/time is finished for me,
though you still journey on
through its leptons and quarks,
remembering in your mind's eye
old days when we were Babylon,
and today marks a cold beginning
of a recall when we flew blue sky
and shared a love's repeating bliss.

I'm gone. Sorry I couldn't kiss
you one last time, hold you, and
give you a last smile to remember.
It's better my leaving on the sly:
loving you from spark to ember,
I could never have said goodbye.

Heroic Crown of Sonnets:
Ancient Chinese Poets

1

Ancient poets were not fooled. In the beginning was the word
carefully chosen to outlast eons, ions, the Table of the Elements,
all of space/time. Nothing exists until it is named, as absurd
as it may seem, for naming gives dimension, mass, and heft
to what our five senses tell us exists outside consciousness—
a deft use of alphabets being the act of creation, the human mind
being reality's library, writing being a slow Big Bang, letters
being subatomic particles, words being thought's molecules aligned.

Ancient poets understood consciousness was the way reality
uses five senses to know itself, show itself, enjoy itself, unite
the physical and the metaphysical, despite the vast banality
of human endeavors. Ancient poets understood space/time
to be merely a tool, a test, a rule at best for a sublime wending,
while words create and destroy chaos from beginning to ending.

2

Tao Chien
365–427

While words create and destroy chaos from beginning to ending
I, a recluse farmer, use few of them, and those I do
tell of poverty, meagerness, brevity, and absence all so true
it's hard to imagine so much of the world not knowing
the plight of human life in the stricture and fixture of space/time,
rivers of life flowing indifferently to the sea's cancellation.
It isn't tomorrow I'm looking for. I stop where I am. No words
can express what is found in emptiness; attempts are a sham.

I farm away my lifetime in anticipation of my consciousness
making sense of suffering in the end, for I am a tethered bird
in space/time's forest, and I sing plaintively to be heard
generations away from this era's striving and arriving at the absurd,
and I respect hunger, and I inspect the empty bowl, for I know
to find sustenance for the soul one must seek absence undeterred.

3

Hsieh Ling-yun
385–433

To find sustenance for the soul one must seek absence undeterred
by the dust of human industry, the clutter of commerce, the utter
collapse of political dicta, religious dogma, and scholars interred
in their libraries. If one is to find sustaining sustenance for the soul,
one must putter and scratch among the green mountains where
earth connects to heaven and heaven to earth, where deep rivers
carry waters from the River of Stars and airy dragons of change
are given birth, where consciousness and absence are given range.

Wilderness is sublime chaos. I write of the erratic twists
and turns of mysterious nature, rivers and mountains, yin and yang,
wilderness never static, always in flux, space/time ever in flow.
My words transcend those of orders and laws, of governments,
of military commands, my poems sending humans an alacrity,
humans needing to speed toward a letting go of human demands.

4

Meng Hao-jan
689–740

Humans needing to speed toward a letting go of human demands
must find freedom from responsibility, independence from wealth,
as I found freedom and independence in vast and unsettled lands,
in high-sky mountains, in cascading rivers wending seaward,
in realizing words hold nothing that isn't better held by silence.
I left unspoken unnecessary things, bold to be silent. I dwelled
rapturously on solar heights where meditation brings absence home,
and I floated mindlessly on the Han River, ever dream-propelled.

I dreamed of nature's gardens instructing me to be still, a theme
of my poems that is not lost on any pilgrims finding their way
through dust of wealth and power, tired, haggard, storm-tossed,
and I encourage followers of the way to step aside, pause, eddy
in the broad streams of life and know the eternal present moment.
They must be ready to relinquish ego and ignore the human absurd.

5

Wang Wei
701–761

They must be ready to relinquish ego and ignore the human absurd,
those who would be awake and aware, serene, content, wisdom-gird.
They must be heady with the elixir derived from leaving out,
letting go, embracing emptiness, concision, silence's icy snow.
I tell you no one can find words to explain finding one's way.
One must climb the mountain oneself, flow along in the river,
experience stones, birds in flight, clouds, and quiver in space/time.
The way is generative, destructive, noun-less, verb-less might.

I say nothing that should not be said, write nothing that should
not be written, finding song in excision, meaning in deletion.
Brevity is long, a word contains volumes, nothing is completion,
and life is not fleshy strands but rather a gong struck once
and its echoes are merely others' memories of our stories.
Only words can remain after our walk on space/time's sands.

6

Li Po
701–762

Only words can remain after our walk on space/time's sands.
I have walked those sands with friends, read my mountain
and rivers poems to them, laughed long in their company,
drank much wine (too much and not enough), wandered lands
threaded by many rivers' waters embedded in wilderness green,
woke to temple bells, aware of temples hidden in hills where
meditation goes on unseen and is none of this world's affair.
I have followed the way hither and thither, here and there.

Don't you know the Silver River of Stars falls through nine skies,
emptying there from where it flows, filling here to where it goes?
I would ride that river from beginning to end, the wilderness,
the moon, and my shadow my only companions, and I would
dance with my shadow, embrace the moon, let go of space/time,
my words arising from the Silver River of Stars and old wine.

7

Tu Fu
712–770

My words arising from the Silver River of Stars and old wine,
they tell of poverty, war, dust, and dragons bringing change.
For decades I wandered the way, not distracted, distraught,
but sure in my being a part of the process, nothing strange
in all that creative chaos of coming and going. I sought
clarity in thought, chose a few jade-hard words to describe
uninhibited roiling and coiling in which space/time is wrought,
words unambiguous in which the essence of being can be caught.

A happy life, seldom a poet's life, is not measured by wealth
or power or fame, but by an ability to be still and experience
good health, drink old wine with one good friend, and thrill
to ancient words now yours to use to help your consciousness ascend
to future generations who read these words and discover ghostly will.
I will watch over space/time flowing toward existence's end.

8

Han Shan
8th Century

I will watch over space/time flowing toward existence's end.
Am I a ghost? Did I ever exist? Was I multiple people
etching a few bone-hard words on stone? Am I immortal?
A legend, yes, but a fiction, too? Clouds of jade mist descend
on Cold Mountain, and I am lost to you. But words are real.
Words are eternal as long as they can be read, infinite in thought
as long as consciousness isn't dead. I send some to you where
you are, where you stand where I stood where the way is sought.

Pilgrim, to know what you are is to know what you are not.
I wrote "impermanence undoes us all," for everything is change,
and if you are crooked then make yourself straight, and if you are
prisoner in your mind's strange thoughts then walk through
meditation's gate to breathe free and be. It's wise to stand apart.
See, taste, hear, smell, and touch should be tools for the heart.

9

Meng Chiao
751–814

See, taste, hear, smell, and touch should be tools for the heart.
Living in desperate times, I used them honestly, accurately to know
yin's feminine darkness, passivity, and yang's masculine show
that dominates with penetrating light—but on my way I found
yin's earth and night more my part of being, not yang's heavenly
might. I was the dark poet, my words painting nature both
ascetic and true. My times with yang's activities were few,
my stark world a reminder of empty oblivion's ability to skew.

I lament all space/time's transient beauty so soon flown
but I also see blossoms drip and drip and drip melting snow,
setting newborn dragons loose, scales glittering, soon known
throughout consciousness as opportunities borne by spring.
Though my words are bitter, opposites are also true and bring
birth, inhalation, awareness, exhalation, dissolution to renew.

10

Po Chu-i
772–846

Birth, inhalation, awareness, exhalation, dissolution to renew
are hallmarks of existence; appearance, disappearance, and I
are one and the same, everything in process, everything true.
My clear words are in an ancient tradition describing chaos
becoming ordered before order collapses back into sheer chaos.
My idle body, empty of action, lies in grass gazing up at clouds.
With nothing on my mind, I am at peace. Away from crowds,
I welcome a reclusive friend as wayward as I. Worries cease.

Words are to be shared not with the world, but with one other.
An ancient pine as reclusive as I also stares skyward, dreams
letting go of the ambient world that, too, is in the flux and flow
of space/time, all of us together would-be, want-to-be friends
who share consciousness and being, my words a call still calling
all these centuries, merely the present stretching for eternity.

11

Li He
790–816

All these centuries, merely the present stretching for eternity,
all these centuries ultimately adding up to emptiness, I live
my own life as a bad-boy poet for later generations to forgive.
Though consciousness is immortal, whatever the mortal body
chooses to do disappears as surely as all space/time disappears
and only words are left to throw wisdom forward past the portal
of death into future minds who will interpret and understand fears
an ancient poet had of culture, wealth, and an authoritarian hand.

I was counted a failure, but not by me. If you are to be a failure,
then be a fine failure. Enjoy. Write. Tell. Point out. Disclose.
Toil away a life? What uselessness! Drink! Have sex! Sing!
My words remain the wisdom of a sot who died young and bring
you much metaphysical food for thought. If you are a fool, laugh.
If you are a tool, be of use. Wise enough to be a bell? Ring!

12

Wang An-shih
1021–1086

If you are a tool, be of use. Wise enough to be a bell? Ring!
I was a tool: prime minister. I was of use, reforming China by
caring for common people, knowing only consciousness is king,
seeing possessions as friction against becoming awake and aware,
daring to challenge prevailing dogma, staring down authority,
and finally retiring to the clarity of wild rivers and mountains
to end my days composing poems that reveal the parity between
control and service, power and submission, the seen and unseen.

My learning in the vast dust of this world I placed in my words.
I experienced presence and absence and know them to be the same.
I realized at last that all of space/time is diminished by its name,
the perennial becoming temporary and the wild becoming tame.
The word both opens and encloses, stops transformation awhile.
The word limits the illimitable so it can be handled and beguile.

13

Su Tung-p'o
1037–1101

The word limits the illimitable so it can be handled and beguile.
Without words, nothing could momentarily detain, slow, or explain
the flow of space/time from oblivion to oblivion, much less send
explanations to future generations. Writers go. Words remain,
they themselves becoming part of the tapestry along the way
of the hundred rivers flowing night and day, all things going
toward oblivion, only the heart refusing the fate of all things clay,
only the heart, in unrequited love with all things, wanting to stay.

Contemplate this: the five senses cannot detect the metaphysical,
the real, the infinite and eternal realms of absence that conceal
origins and destinations which words gallantly attempt to let us feel,
taste, smell, hear, and see. Each consciousness is locked inside
itself until death, each consciousness in perpetuity on a ride.
Sliding toward oblivion calls for words to record every mile.

14

Shihwu
1272–1352

Sliding toward oblivion calls for words to record every mile.
In my few words, I've told you about space/time's flow.
What more can be said about poverty, absence, solitude,
life, and love that you don't already know? Open your heart
and look in there. Open your mind. Empty it. Search
for desolate places. The world isn't unkind, it just doesn't
care. Know in the process of everything you play a part.
Safe in yourself, rest assured no one knows you're there.

I am a hermit beyond praise or blame and I burn candles
to see to write a much greater flame. I light my life. Do you
light yours? I eat porridge, eschew fine foods. Some think me
a simpleton and find my koans absurd, but those who read me
when in their meditative moods will not be passion-ruled.
Ancient poets were not fooled. In the beginning was the word.

15

Ancient poets were not fooled. In the beginning was the word.
While words create and destroy chaos from beginning to ending,
to find sustenance for the soul one must seek absence undeterred.
Humans needing to speed toward a letting go of human demands,
they must be ready to relinquish ego and ignore the human absurd.
Only our words can remain after our walk on space/time's sands.
My words arising from the Silver River of Stars and old wine,
I will watch over space/time flowing toward existence's end.

See, taste, hear, smell, and touch should be tools for the heart.
Birth, inhalation, awareness, exhalation, dissolution to renew
all these centuries, merely the present stretching for eternity.
If you are a tool, be of use. Wise enough to be a bell? Ring!
The word limits the illimitable so it can be handled and beguile.
Sliding toward oblivion calls for words to record every mile.

Acknowledgment

The poem "It's Not Dementia" first appeared in *The Healing Muse*.

Title Index

A

Adagio for Alpenhorns 74
Adagio for a Young Cousin 93
Adagio for the Oort Cloud 102
Adagio for Timpani 85
A Dragon Speaks 72
A Good Day 27
Ambient Air 39
... And They Lived Happily Ever After 133
Angst Astride a Dragon 83
Ars Moriendi 101
Auld Lang Syne 130

B

Beatitude 1 45
Beatitude 2 47
Beatitude 3 48
Beatitude 4 49
Beatitude 5 50
Beatitude 6 52
Beatitude 7 54
Beatitude 8 55
Before Dust Settled 87
Being in a Garden 116

C

Centripetal Versus Centrifugal 78
Congenital Myopia 109
Consciousness on the Way 61
Coronavirus 37
COVID-19 60

D

Disbelief 58
Dragonfly 99
Dust and Dragons 15
Dusting 104
Dust Mites 42
Dust Versus Dragons 19

G

Gold Dust 91
Great Misery Island, Salem Harbor, Massachusetts 30

H

Heroic Crown of Sonnets:
    Ancient Chinese Poets 135
Hey, Billy 92
Hymn to Yesterday's Gods 125

I

I Am Who I Am 66
Idleness 80
I, Dragon 56
Immortality 115
I'm Tidying Up Things
    With My Grandmother Again 81
Incarnations 106
Intellect as Companion 122
It's Not Dementia 128

K

Koan 33

L

Last Illusions 124
Love in Time 32

M

May You Live in Interesting Times 41
Memory of a Shadow of a Fog 88
Milky Way 69
My Boyfriend is an Asian Dragon 35
My Grandmother Busies Herself in My Kitchen 62

O

Old in a Dust Storm 95
Once Upon a Time 17
On Your Finding I'm Gone 134
Orbis Non Sufficit 70
Our Role 22

P

Purgatory 121

R

Rubáiyát 20

S

Sequel 96
Simplification 65
Spring Dreams in Autumn 97
Stardust 36

T

Thacher Island, Rockport, Massachusetts 23
There Be Dragons 64
. . . They Moved Together
    Through Dust and Dragons 43
Those Who Knew Me
    When My World Was Young 111

V
Voices 25

W
What If It Comes as a Sleeping? 132
What Will He Get? 90
Why the Night Sky Is Dark 67
Winter Dragon 113
World Inside 29

Y
Youth's Departure 108

First Line Index

A

All outside of flesh is only ambience to consciousness 29
A massive old year passes with banked fires 130
Ancient poets were not fooled.
   In the beginning was the word 135
And may you be granted a long life ensconced 41
And so I have come to here and now 124
And so snow-like dust, settled on
   the frozen lake of human ambition 60
And so with the winter solstice the lake freezes over 113
And we did indeed, dying slowly as we all die 133
And what an art it is, this dying, this slow turning away 101
An old photograph brushes dust from memory 87

B

Before life, like afterlife, beggars belief 88
Being nothing goes with doing nothing 80
But I could've loved you, would've, too 45
But one by one my friends fell away
   from our reality's beauty 58

D

Decades (too many) separate us from being buddies 93

E

Early morning, and this past spring's fawns champ grass 74
Even this winter dies. Even blank, clammy January 70
Even what I've finished remains incomplete 95

F

For the life of me, I can't get used to seeing old friends 128

G

Granite shelves rising to just below 23

H

Here with you in your aging's private wilderness 122
He wants a lot . . . and all of it fleeting, fleeing time 90
Hey, Billy, did you ever think we'd be this old? 92
Holiday's here again, and again I won't cook 62
How simple can I get? Jettisoning
   experiences right and left 65
Human doubting, flouting, outing, pouting, routing 39

I

I can see my breath so I know it's cold; only the 81
I let you go. Take love away from where I lie 54
Ill and old, ill and old, I see daffodils yellow still 99
I look away— down, in fact, in submission to you 48
I love innocently when I can, guiltily when I can't 52
I'm connected to my yesterday self, yesteryear self 115
In being's last chapter, I look back 97
In my bedroom's midnight quiet, I hear them 25
In my sodden, quiet, quite terminal December 109
Innumerable darknesses of immemorial night 83
I recreate my history more to my liking, the way 61
Is it cancer, death, lost love, divorce, poverty? 72
It is spring, kind of like spring, some form of spring 35
I, too, do not know from where I came. I hover shivering 56
I turn to find your cardigan folded as you left it 91
It will leave, spring, the way youth leaves 108
It won't always be now, there coming a time 50
I've walked below high-tide lines on childhood's beaches 33

J

Jan Oort knew something of how quickly from nothing 102

L

Little darling daring to rule the planet 37
Living in dust, thriving in dust, creating dust 42
Love plies like life plies, languidly, a day at a time 47
Lovers (and who are more persecuted than they?) 55

M

May this day come ad nauseam 27
My grandmother taught me how to dust 104

N

Not as a gunshot? Not as a knife thrust 132

R

Real, suddenly, they are: these sunlit plants 116
Ruffling through memory, shuffling dust of experience 106

S

Sometimes in late evening, or early morning 111
So what do I do, I who hunger, thirst? I watch you 49
Space/time, from its inception through to its demise 32
Space/time is finished for me 134
Stars all unthought of, let alone unseen 67

T

Thank you. You filled the bill until we came 125
The Big Bang of my birth exploded a universe 17
The dust we kick up in our blitherings and ditherings 19
The river of space/time flows on and away 20
The script that youth writes is bold, smooth, sharply lined 96
These forces are part of the flow of space/time 78
The wiggly lines twirl stupendously 69
They lie awakening at the bottom of still waters 64
Throughout space/time it falls, coming down 15

W

We have arrived at planet Earth, our destination 22
What were they, those days both blue and gold? 36
When we began loving each other, we were naïve, glad 43
Who hasn't, long ago, heard sonorous, stentorian thunder roll 85
Wind is unaware of who I am. Unknown am I 66
With beers he stole from his father's stash 30

Y

You see an old man as he is: frail, flaccid, failing 121

www.ingramcontent.com/pod-product-compliance
Lightning Source LLC
Chambersburg PA
CBHW010051200426
43193CB00059B/2922